best of education & culture

INTERIOR DESIGN BEST OF EDUCATION & CULTURE

EDITOR IN CHIEF
Cindy Allen

EXECUTIVE EDITOR
Jen Renzi

BOOKS EDITOR
Georgina McWhirter

SENIOR DESIGNER
Karla Lima

DESIGNERS
Selena Chen
Melissa Kaufmann

SENIOR EDITOR
Kathryn Daniels

MANAGING EDITOR
Helene E. Oberman

CONTRIBUTING WRITERS
Mairi Beautyman
Edie Cohen
Kelly Hushin
Craig Kellogg
Mark McMenamin
C.C. Sullivan
Nicholas Tamarin

PREPRESS IMAGING SPECIALIST
Igor Tsiperson

PRODUCTION
Sarah Dentry
Kay Kojima
Dana Rouse

BOOKS DIRECTOR
Kathy Harrigan

MARKETING DIRECTOR
Tina Brennan

MARKETING ART DIRECTOR
Denise Figueroa

Library of Congress Control Number 2014946572
ISBN-13: 978-0-9833263-5-9
Printed in China
10 9 8 7 6 5 4 3 2 1

INTERIOR DESIGN®

INTERIOR DESIGN MEDIA
1271 Avenue of the Americas, 17th Floor, New York, NY 10020
www.interiordesign.net

SANDOW
Corporate Headquarters
3651 NW 8th Avenue, Boca Raton, FL 33431
www.sandow.com

foreword
by Cindy Allen

Who couldn't use a little more culture—or learning—in their lives? My dad (a knowledge monger, I called him) was a former math professor teaching in the New York City school system. While curating this book, I got sentimental, thinking of him and the rickety old classrooms that became his other home. Boy, would he have loved to shape young minds in any of the groundbreaking spaces shown in these pages! And what I'd give to have grown up in a time when my school, library, or even local movie theater was "designed," with the end user (me) in mind.

I am therefore delighted to present *Interior Design Best of Education & Culture*, the latest edition in our expanding series. Institutions of learning, places of worship, summer camps, and science labs have hardly been considered hotbeds of innovation...until now, and our Universe Study backs that up. From 2011 to 2013, revenue from cultural projects more than doubled, from $32 million to $68 million. Of the total 30,439 firms in our industry, 42 percent work on educational projects (who knew?). And the head count? A whopping 64,000 designers.

The projects may vary, but all aim to foster community and enrich the lives of their occupants (don't even *think* of asking how many!). Some are low tech, like the pavilion and boathouse design for an

Upper Manhattan flood zone—a model of sustainability engineered to stand strong in the event of another Sandy—meant to nurture children's environmental concerns. It's hard to go higher tech than the futuristic Nanchang cinema, featured on our cover, where, mystifyingly, nothing is as it seems. Of course we celebrate such green projects as the offbeat, off-the-grid wooden-egg dwelling moored in imperiled UK coastland that turns out to be the resident-artist's statement on the natural world.

Some especially generous souls donate their time and talent to give back to the community. Take *Interior Design* Hall of Famer—and this year's Pritzker prize winner— Shigeru Ban, an "emergency architecture" specialist whose interim, earthquake-proof cathedral is made of cardboard, with faux stained-glass windows, no less.

My dad Algray would've gone particularly bonkers, I think, over the Antarctic research station parked on a melting ice shelf. (The hydraulic legs on this eight-module caravan allow it to stay a step ahead of rising snow; attached skis make towing the whole unit a breeze; and did we mention the Pierre Paulin lounge chairs?) But if Dad were around today, I'm sure he'd give each of these projects *a resounding A+.*

best of education & culture
contents

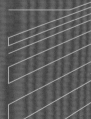

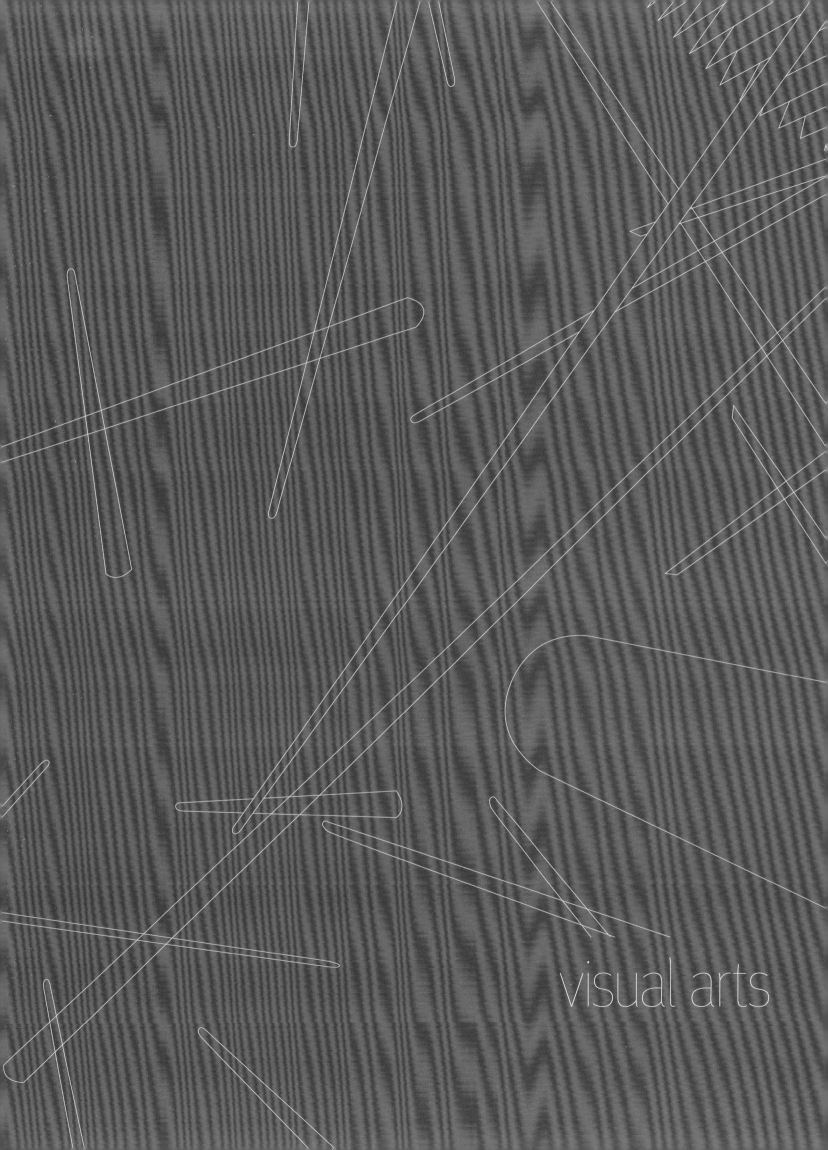

visual arts

Talk about mixed media: A majority
of these visual-arts spaces are
intriguing cross-disciplinary hybrids.

There's a museum/hotel, a cinema/bookstore, an installation/houseboat, and an art-fair VIP lounge as sly social commentary. Forget the white-box archetype; these richly layered and nuanced spaces are as evocative as the works on display. Even in the most traditional of gallery environments, where a neutral backdrop is still de rigueur, staircases and circulation spaces provide opportunities for expressive architecture—strident moves to sculpt space that become sculptures in their own right. *A fine art indeed.*

Elliott + Associates Architects

ADKINS GALLERY AND STUART WING, FRED JONES JR. MUSEUM OF ART
UNIVERSITY OF OKLAHOMA, NORMAN

Clockwise from above: Next to the central staircase, a pillar with see-through cutouts—a riff on a steel column—elevates a construction detail to fine art. Encircling the museum's top floor is a ribbon of green glass, a nod to the peaked slate rooftops of the neighboring Lester Wing. Wheeled walls abet reconfiguration, giving curators flexibility in displaying the museum's extensive holdings of Southwestern and Native American artworks. ➤

Designing a museum is tricky business. The architecture should neither compete with the art it houses nor be too self-effacing. A catch-22? Not for Rand Elliott, who makes crafting an intriguing blank canvas (an oxymoron if ever there was one) look easy in his firm's renovation and expansion of this university art museum.

The project, winner of a coveted American Architecture Award, more than doubled the gallery space: It went from 18,000 to 40,000 square feet...on a shoestring budget, no less. Inside and out, inspiration came from colors and forms found in paintings, photography, and artifacts from the institution's Eugene B. Adkins Collection, a leading private archive of Native American art. The glass on the building facade reflects the cloudscape above while alluding to the sky paintings on display in the galleries—a subtle teaser of what's to come.

Inside, a new central staircase features wood sidewalls that recall a canyon in the Southwest. Thick mobile partitions used to reconfigure exhibition spaces took inspiration from adobe. And water, a recurring motif in the collections, sparked a star attraction: a spectacular blue moiré wall that rises through all three stories.

Clockwise from left: Lighting, fire protection, alarm systems, and HVAC are concealed in ceiling slots. White oak floors throughout create a seamless transition between old and new. The Adkins Gallery. Rising three stories, the 55-foot-wide moiré screen animates the staircase like an aqueous scrim. Stair treads are white oak. Proportions, wall thickness, and scale were carefully conceived to create a harmonious space.

54,570 sf
8,300 sf Adkins Gallery
4,500 sf photography gallery
$13 million budget

PROJECT TEAM RAND ELLIOTT, MIKE MAYS, MICHAEL SHUCK
CM AT RISK MANHATTAN CONSTRUCTION COMPANY
CIVIL ENGINEER SMITH ROBERTS BALDISCHWILER
STRUCTURAL ENGINEER EUDALEY ENGINEERS
MEP ENGINEER DETERMAN SCHEIRMAN
PHOTOGRAPHY SCOTT McDONALD/HEDRICH BLESSING
www.e-a-a.com

1 MAIN STAIRCASE

2 ADKINS GALLERY

3 LIGHT WELL

4 ART SCHOOL

5 STORAGE

6 FREIGHT ELEVATOR

7 RESTROOMS

8 OFFICES

9 LOBBY

0 10 20   40

One Plus Partnership

NANCHANG INSUN INTERNATIONAL CINEMA
NANCHANG, CHINA

These days, a best seller invariably begets a movie, and fans of the book can only hope nothing major is lost in translation. This cinema, fittingly set in a bookstore, took a cue from the literary world and pulled off an Oscar-worthy adaptation. The cashiers' desks in the lobby, reminiscent of stacks of paper, are actually milled solid-surfacing. Posters for current films are displayed on white powdercoated-steel planes that fan out like the pages of a script. Structural columns are clad in a marble whose striations evoke a hardback's deckle edges.

Taking the reference a step further (as paper is made from trees), design directors Ajax Law Ling Kit and Virginia Lung devised long tubular light fixtures that angle down from the ceiling like the lifted limbs of a tree; a green powdercoating enhances the verdant vibe. The ceiling is painted black, a color that also engulfs a corridor branching off the lobby. Scattered across inky walls are, in various colors and fonts, snippets of dialogue from *The Curious Case of Benjamin Button*—a prime incarnation of the book-to-movie metamorphosis.

From above:
Silkscreened dialogue from a popular Hong Kong movie adorns a corridor. The lobby's custom steel lighting fixtures stretch 18 to 24 feet long.

78,500 sf
9 theaters
Interior Design 2013 Best of Year Winner, Common Space

"When you set foot inside, you can hardly tell it's a cinema. We camouflaged everything under the mask of different materials. Even the concession counter blends with the background so well, it takes time to notice its existence" —AJAX LAW LING KIT

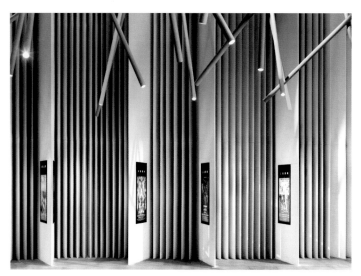

Clockwise from top:
Cashiers' desks in milled solid-surfacing mimic stacks of paper. Powdercoated-steel fins detail the gift shop. Some 100 light fixtures animate the lobby. LED lighting punctuates the corridor leading to the nine theaters. Posters for upcoming movies are inserted into thin sheaths of steel that resemble pages of a book. ➤

"You could be mad as a mad
at the way things went you car
sweat and curse the fates,
but when it comes to the
you have

1 LOBBY
2 THEATERS
3 RESTROOM
4 VIP LOUNGE

PROJECT TEAM AJAX LAW LING KIT, VIRGINIA LUNG
PHOTOGRAPHY JONATHAN LEIJONHUFVUD

www.onepluspartnership.com

Clockwise from opposite: An angular polyester-upholstered theater wall. Strips of fabric cover the walls and ceiling of another theater. Standard cinema seating sports custom covers.

PAD Studio and SPUD Group

EXBURY EGG, BEAULIEU RIVER
LYMINGTON, HAMPSHIRE, ENGLAND

Stephen Turner might never have moved into an egg if he hadn't nearly crushed one while exploring an estuary on the tidal Beaulieu River—one of the few privately owned rivers in the world. That was when the installation artist found his boot perilously close to the pale-blue shell of a herring gull's egg. The experience, he says, made him "consider the preciousness of all life attempting to make a home in a changing landscape where humans are the greatest threat."

Disaster averted, Turner got an idea he then pitched to SPUD Group (short for Space Placemaking and Urban Design), an organization that supports architects and artists who want to raise ecological awareness: "You know what? I'd like to live in an egg." His brief called for an off-the-grid, low-tech houseboat that would symbolize fragility. Another SPUD collaborator, PAD Studio director Wendy Perring, put a design to Turner's vision and a local boatbuilder executed it. The result was a frame of circular plywood fins and Douglas fir stringers; the timber strips sandwiched a fiberglass shell.

At high tide, the egg stays upright thanks to full water tanks at its base; during low tide, it rests on steel concrete-filled feet. Turner, meanwhile, sleeps in a hammock and works at a built-in tabletop, recording his day-to-day experiences via interactive webcam and drawings—his nest securely tethered to a pontoon just feet from that life-altering encounter with a gull's egg.

A wooden shell floating in a British estuary serves as an artist's temporary home and studio while drawing attention to threatened coastal marshland. ➤

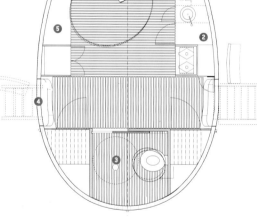

```
0    5   10        20
```

1 LIVING/SLEEPING AREA

2 KITCHENETTE

3 SHOWER

4 ENTRY

5 TABLETOP

Clockwise from above: Untreated western red cedar composes the egg's exterior. Repurposed Douglas fir, western red cedar, and pine creates a striped effect inside the shell. Punctuating the structure are two round skylights and two rectangular doors with radiused corners. The shower area. A test launch. For its 16-mile journey from the shipyard, the egg was transported on local roads to avoid highway overpasses. ➤

12 by 20 feet
1½ tons

"Our brief called for an off-the-grid, low-tech structure that an artist could use as a part-time live/work space. The egg symbolizes fragility and the cycle of life" —SPUD PRINCIPAL ASSOCIATE MARK DRURY

MARITIME ENGINEER PFJ MARITIME CONSULTING
WOODWORK BEAU WOOD STRUCTURES
PHOTOGRAPHY NIGEL RIGDEN

www.padstudio.co.uk
www.spudgroup.org.uk

21c MUSEUM HOTEL, BENTONVILLE, ARKANSAS

Deborah Berke Partners

When is a hotel more than a hotel? When, like the 21c Museum Hotel, it comes with its own contemporary art gallery—one open to the public free of charge 24 hours a day, 7 days a week. This quirky arrangement was the brainchild of Laura Lee Brown and Steve Wilson, who founded the brand in 2006 with the guiding tenet that art should be part of everyday life.

Rather than editing a historic building's personality—as the architecture firm did with its first two 21c hotels, in Louisville and Cincinnati—Deborah Berke Partners was able to build from the ground up here. Berke seized the opportunity, creating open, light-filled spaces that speak to the flexibility and reach of the hybrid program. A large one-story street-front wing houses public functions; a multilevel structure behind it accommodates guests. That configuration allowed the architect to invite natural light into the public spaces several ways: A clerestory illuminates the lobby, floor-to-ceiling windows line a gallery facing the street, and a courtyard punctuates the restaurant.

Public areas reiterate the urban-gallery language through high ceilings, white walls, and polished-concrete floors. In each of the 100-plus guestrooms, a neutral palette provides the backdrop for the artworks. Among the most thought-provoking of the latter: Daan Roosegaarde's *Flow 5.0*, a wall of fans which respond to sound and movement, and *Tree of 40 Fruit* by artist/master arborist Sam Van Aken, which produces multiple varieties of stone fruit.

Clockwise from opposite: *Artist Anne Peabody used an aluminum-on-glass printing process to create* Hide and Seek, *a forest of translucent trees on walls and doors in a restroom vestibule. The lobby gallery is illuminated via a clerestory, while the street-front gallery is brightened by full-height fenestration. In the Hive restaurant, custom screens made of ash slats display works from the museum collection.* ➤

Clockwise from opposite top: Animating the pre-function gallery is Serkan Özkaya's A Sudden Gust of Wind, *composed of 400 metal sheets calling to mind a maelstrom of paper. In the Art Yard, Alexandre Arrechea's Orange Tree—which sprouts "branches" of basketball hoops—explores the relationship between sports and urban street culture. Making a wry statement in the gym is Virginie Barré's Fat Bat (in polyurethane foam, resin, and cloth). The iron-spot clay-brick facade. A custom canopy of hemlock slats defines the lobby gallery.*

1 MAIN GALLERY

2 PRE-FUNCTION GALLERY

3 RESTAURANT

4 BAR

5 ENTRY

6 LOBBY GALLERY

7 BOARDROOM

8 VIDEO GALLERY

9 MEETING ROOM

10 ART YARD

0 20 40   80

PROJECT TEAM DEBORAH BERKE, FAIA, LEED AP; STEPHEN BROCKMAN, LEED AP;
TERRENCE SCHROEDER, LEED AP
PHOTOGRAPHY TIMOTHY HURSLEY (1–5, 7, 8), RETT PEEK (6)

www.dberke.com
www.21cmuseumhotels.com

5,155 sf
$5,500 project cost

Mayfield
and Ragni
Studio

TEXAS CONTEMPORARY ART FAIR 2012
VIP LOUNGE, HOUSTON

Click on the Culture page of MaRS's website and the cheerful likenesses of founder-principals Kelie Mayfield and Erick Ragni slowly morph into green-skinned aliens with antennae. That brand of irreverence earned the recently established Houston design firm the VIP lounge commission at the 2012 Texas Contemporary Art Fair. "To answer the phone 'Welcome to MaRS' is quite enjoyable," says Mayfield with a grin. "We try to include humor in every job; seriousness is sufficiently covered in the marketplace." Take the studio's use of exercise balls, bound together to form ottomans—it's a nod to the ongoing campaign to transform Houston's reputation as one of the fattest cities in the United States. Or the typographic feature wall reminiscent of the lightbulb signs that used to animate honky-tonks in small Texas towns. One major challenge was to create an intimate space in a cavernous convention hall. A grid of 24 umbrellas tempered the 35-foot ceiling—and slyly referenced another Houston ranking: as America's sixth rainiest city.

PROJECT TEAM KELIE MAYFIELD, ERICK RAGNI,
BECKY HARRISON, RUDY FABRE
PHOTOGRAPHY ERIC LAIGNEL
www.marsculture.com

Clockwise from above: An Ann Wood installation of flower- and pom-pom-encrusted sheep anchored one corner of the lounge. Exercise balls were fashioned into seating units using suction cups, glue, and zip ties. Two 16-foot-long walls made of ¾-inch foam board beckoned patrons to complete sentences starting "Art is..." and "Texas is..." with china markers. Umbrellas, nylon carpet tile, and repurposed shipping pallets—all donated, like MaRS's design services—defined the VIP lounge. Cable spools served as tables.

Desai Chia Architecture

LUMINOUS DEPTHS
PERANAKAN MUSEUM, SINGAPORE

When artist Lee Mingwei called Desai Chia Architecture, it was with an unusual request: for the firm to design a structure not to protect his art but to protect people *from* his art. The proposed installation, *Luminous Depths*, would be on display at Singapore's Peranakan Museum, an ethnographic institution devoted to the local blended culture. Visitors could buy white ceramic vessels and carry them up to the third level of an atrium; standing on a ceremonial platform built for the purpose, they'd then toss them over a balustrade to the marble floor below.

"It's about release," Katherine Chia says. Mingwei adds, "Breaking from daily experience invites possibility into life. And that can be hard to do."

Such cathartic anarchy may seduce, but practical safety protocols had to be considered. Partners Chia and Arjun Desai minimized the risk of the high-velocity objects' shattering by installing a lightweight protective frame in the atrium: a snow-white basketball hoop and net to control the airborne vessels' trajectory. Aircraft cable strung from four corner columns supported a series of steel rings interconnected via rope. At the top, transparent vinyl and a tight web of bird netting provided insurance against errant throws; at the bottom, tall panels of frosted acrylic contained ricocheting shards. The resulting structure was minimal and elegant—an artwork in itself.

Clockwise from above: Luminous Depths *was installed in the central atrium of Singapore's Peranakan Museum. The four rings, of painted steel, ranged from 7 to 15 feet in diameter. To capture shards at the bottom of the atrium, an enclosure was built with acrylic panels. The rope structure measured 36 feet high. The vertical nylon rope overlaid by bird netting. Ceramics in the museum collection inspired the shapes of vessels available for tossing.*

800 sf

PROJECT TEAM KATHERINE CHIA, ARJUN DESAI
ARTIST LEE MINGWEI
GENERAL CONTRACTOR SPACELOGIC
PHOTOGRAPHY KATHERINE CHIA (1, 2, 4), SANDY SHIN WONG (3, 5), ISSA WENG (6)
www.desaichia.com

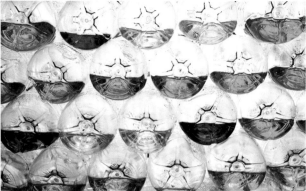

HEAD IN THE CLOUDS, GOVERNORS ISLAND, NEW YORK

StudioKCA

Composed of
53,780 recycled bottles

Clockwise from bottom: StudioKCA's temporary pavilion on Governors Island was crafted from recycled bottles. Visitors flocked to the installation, a commentary on the more than 60 million plastic bottles discarded daily in the United States. Water tinted with blue food coloring filled the vessels lining the interior.

As Governors Island prepared to host the Figment arts festival under Lady Liberty's sidelong gaze, an AIA New York Chapter competition solicited plans for a temporary pavilion. The prompt: What would an art pavilion made out of recycled materials and based around the idea of a "City of Dreams" look like to you?

StudioKCA principals Jason Klimoski and Lesley Chang won the opportunity to build their fanciful first-place entry, *Head in the Clouds*, then went straight to Kickstarter for funding—and collected 100 percent. They also collected 53,780 used plastic water bottles and milk jugs, approximately the number of empties the city discards in a single hour, with help from 200 volunteers. Preassembled sections of the "cloud" were ferried over from Manhattan via water taxi and attached with metal wire to an aluminum armature 40 feet long. White translucent jugs formed the outer surface, while smaller transparent bottles lined the inside. The latter contained varying amounts of liquid in shades of blue, a combination of water and food coloring, creating a painterly dreamscape.

PROJECT TEAM JASON KLIMOSKI, LESLEY CHANG, BRIAN CHU, JINWON LEE, JOSETTE MATTHEW, HECTOR ORELLANA, CORY ZWERLEIN
PHOTOGRAPHY CHUCK CHOI
www.studiokca.com

Moneo Brock Studio and Quanto Arquitectura

ESPACIO FUNDACIÓN TELEFÓNICA, MADRID

You could be forgiven for thinking the Cor-Ten-covered tentacles winding around and through the helical staircase at the Espacio Fundación Telefónica gallery were part of a temporary installation. But quite the contrary: the biomorphic forms are load-bearing. They support a four-level section of facade that was cut free from the rest of the landmark Telefónica headquarters, creating an ample stair atrium to welcome visitors (it also doubles as a fire exit in an emergency).

The Cor-Ten bracing can be seen through the stair's glass balustrades, its bolts echoing the rivets on the 1929 building's columns. The twisty supports are brought as close as possible to the stair's spiral, producing a captivating gesture at the gallery entrance. "The staircase lets people on the street know immediately," says Moneo Brock's Belén Moneo Feduchi, "that they are on their way to somewhere important." Elsewhere, oak trim contrasts with painted steel-mesh ceiling panels and polished-concrete floors. All materials were chosen to recede in the presence of paintings by Joan Miró and Eduardo Chillida, cubist works, adventure photography, and installations. In addition to exhibitions, there's a café, children's workshops, education areas, and an amphitheater-style auditorium.

At the Espacio Fundación Telefónica, cross-bracing clad in Cor-Ten steel intersects with a spiral staircase. ➤

MONEO BROCK STUDIO BÉLEN MONEO FEDUCHI, ANDRÉS BARRÓN, MARÍA PIERRES, ALBERT RUBIO

QUANTO ARQUITECTURA SUSANA TORRE ARIAS, DIANA DO RÍO, VICTORIA CORTÉS LAHUERTA, REBECA SARABIA PICAZO, ANDRÉS DAZA PABÓN, ALEJANDRA OCHOA FERRER, ENRIQUE BONET

ACOUSTICAL CONSULTANT DECIBEL INGENIEROS

STRUCTURAL ENGINEER NB35

GLASSWORK UNIÓN VIDRIERA GRUPO

STEELWORK BEPAES, GRUPSA

GENERAL CONTRACTOR SANJOSE CONSTRUCTORA

PHOTOGRAPHY COURTESY OF MONEO BROCK STUDIO (1, 4, 5), LUIS ASÍN (2, 3, 6)

www.moneobrock.com
www.quantoarquitectura.com

1 MAIN ENTRANCE

2 STAIRCASE

3 LOBBY

4 ELEVATOR

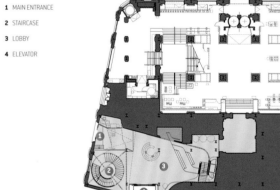

0 10 20   40

Clockwise from left:
In the gallery, original riveted steel columns were coated with a fire retardant and painted a lustrous silver. The staircase connects ground level to three stories above. Stainless-steel handrails are bolted to balustrades of laminated glass. Cove lighting is LED. Quanto Arquitectura designed the lobby.

69,000 sf

TEXAS CONTEMPORARY ART FAIR 2013
VIP LOUNGE, HOUSTON

After creating a much-buzzed-about VIP lounge for the 2012 installment of this annual art fair, Mayfield and Ragni Studio was invited back for a sophomore turn. Once again the firm delivered, with an experiential space conceived to extend the enjoyment of thought-provoking artworks.

To embody their chosen themes—which included a nod to the state's largest export, oil—MaRS collaborated with Woreman Brand Agency to design a quartet of tongue-in-cheek wall coverings. One graphic depicted a kaleidoscopic print of gym-goers on exercise balls surrounded by ice cream cones. (Viewed from afar, the designers note, the distinctive latticework motif resembles magnified fat cells.) Printed in positive and negative, the patterns were used to line partitions defining the room's perimeter.

Roche Bobois' low-slung Mah Jong seating gave tired attendees a spot to rest while enjoying a prime view of a quirky installation by Katja Loher. For the project, the Swiss-born artist projected her video art, in which words were spelled out using images of posed dancers, on weather balloons overhead. Visitors urged (by signage) to view other videos through a peephole found their eye similarly superimposed on a balloon: a sly take on modern surveillance. And a 30-foot-long lounge table anchoring the space became a canvas for yet another offbeat projection—this time, of food and drink—cast on dinner plates and inside carafes and wineglasses, respectively, further blurring the line between art and reality.

Mayfield and Ragni Studio

Clockwise from right: The temporary lounge was Mayfield and Ragni Studio's second for the annual art fair. Demarcating the rear bar was a partition studded with bottle openers on a background of red, the event's signature color. Black-and-white wall coverings featured graphic interpretations of Texan themes. Floor tiles donated the previous year by Shaw Contract were used in a new pattern, part of the firm's commitment to sustainable practice. The curious who took a look through this peephole had an image of their eyeball projected on a nearby balloon. Roche Bobois contributed all the seating, and Caesarstone, the solid surfacing. Video footage projected on a tabletop simulated a laden dinner plate.

4,150 sf

PROJECT TEAM KELIE MAYFIELD, ERICK RAGNI, BECKY HARRISON, RUDY FABRE
PHOTOGRAPHY ERIC LAIGNEL

www.marsculture.com

28,000 sf
$12.6 million project cost

Do historical collections demand traditional architecture? Should facades be backward-looking billboards to advertise the exhibitions housed inside? In conceiving this hybrid building, Trey Trahan responded to both questions with a resounding "No way!" But then he had to persuade the authorities of the oldest city in the Louisiana Purchase. Queries and concerns persisted, since the museum would house both sports and regional-history collections. Were dual architectural identities required for the multitasking facility? Trahan dissented once again. Sports memories, he argued, are just one more component of regional culture.

A stridently contemporary tone is set the moment patrons enter the atrium lobby. Here, sunlight from above washes white cast-stone panels in curves that evoke the dynamic surface of the Cane River Lake, a spring-training mecca for crew teams. Visitors to a veranda on the building's top level see the historic town square from behind copper louvers; the pleated facade panels are likewise copper. And as modern as the architecture might initially appear, Trahan points out, the louvers and panels allude to the classic shutters and clapboards of the state's plantations.

Clockwise from opposite: Skylights illuminate the interior of the museum, located on the banks of the Cane River. The rectilinear copper-panel facade belies the sinuous forms inside. Undulating walls reflect the river's meandering path. ➤

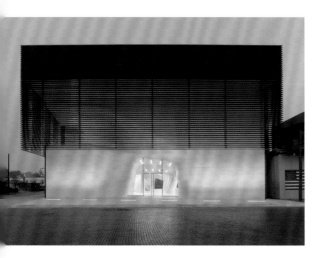

Trahan Architects

LOUISIANA SPORTS HALL OF FAME & NORTHWEST LOUISIANA HISTORY MUSEUM NATCHITOCHES, LOUISIANA

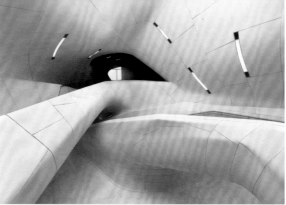

Clockwise from below: Over 1,000 digitally milled cast-stone panels form the building's interior. Walls function as screens for video exhibits. The spaces flow both visually and physically. A swooping staircase connects ground-level galleries and classrooms to a veranda overlooking the city. Exhibits explore the connection between sports and regional history.

1 CLASSROOM

2 FOYER

3 GALLERY

4 VERANDA

0   10   20   40

PROJECT TEAM BRAD McWHIRTER, ED GASKIN, MARK HASH, MICHAEL McCUNE,
SEAN DAVID, BLAKE FISHER, ERIK HERRMANN, DAVID MERLIN, BENJAMIN RATH,
JUDSON TERRY
PHOTOGRAPHY TIMOTHY HURSLEY

www.trahanarchitects.com

performing arts

By the time you enter one of these performing-arts venues—which range from concert halls to rehearsal spaces—the theatrical experience is well under way.

Structures of striking beauty and utility, they use glazing, technology, lighting, and outsize typography to beckon visitors and invite an interdisciplinary dialogue.

A theater lobby flashes snippets of Shakespeare via LEDs. A new incubator for emerging theater talent was built right atop an Eero Saarinen structure. One facility unites a university's music, dance, and drama departments: a glass-wall rehearsal studio cantilevered over grass makes dancers feel suspended in air—while those outside take in tantalizing views of artists at work. *Is that a standing ovation we hear?*

Clockwise from right:
Lit by a clerestory, a stairwell wall showcases photographs of student performers by Joe Aker printed on brushed-aluminum panels. Bench-style modular units in the 7,000-square-foot lobby, which features stretching areas for dance students, playing spots for music students, and informal rehearsal space for theater students. One of the four 2,100-square-foot dance studios. ➤

"No square boxes!" was the demand of this client, a top-ranked performing-arts school seeking to unite its previously dispersed music, dance, and theater departments. The goal was a space that would foster creative cross-pollination while evoking emotions as potent as the performances to be held within. Rising to the occasion, WHR gracefully cantilevered four second-floor dance studios over the ground level, creating high drama while maximizing the compact site. Another clever coup was the resolution of the sloped-ground situation: The architects tucked an outdoor performance area into the site's steepest part, forming terraces that gently bridged the 18-foot grade change and provided additional seating as well.

The interior is as sensitively conceived as the elegant facade. Angular elements suggestive of movement—for one, the modular seating zigzagging through lofty breakout areas—soften the architecture's orthogonality. And to break the gridlike rigidity of ceramic- and resilient-tile floors, the team devised a quirky design statement, carrying bars and blocks of color underfoot and up the walls: a treatment that works to mediate shifts between differently scaled spaces. WHR didn't shy away from a little sparkle, either. Quartz tiles with glittery flecks spice up typically bland utilitarian surfaces like restroom countertops and walls by drinking fountains. Out of the box indeed.

WHR
Architects

JAMES AND NANCY GAERTNER
PERFORMING ARTS CENTER
SAM HOUSTON STATE UNIVERSITY
HUNTSVILLE, TEXAS

1 RECITAL HALL

2 CONCERT HALL

3 LOBBY

4 OFFICE BLOCK

5 THEATER REHEARSAL STUDIOS

6 DANCE THEATER

0 20 40   80

"Dance studios were cantilevered over the first floor by necessity, but they also reinforce a sense of dance through flight, helping dancers experience the feeling of being aloft" —WHR ARCHITECTS

The space for practice juts over the lawn and seemingly into the sky. ➤

Clockwise from right:
Multiple layers of cost-effective drywall—treated to color-blocked paint—were used in sound-critical spaces and performance areas, such as the 160-seat dance theater. Daylight enters a dance studio through north-facing full-height glazing. Maple-veneer treatments in the 182-seat recital hall unify upper and lower seating levels while masking ductwork above balconies. A glass sculpture by Jason Lawson is displayed in a hallway. Maple-veneer panels hung from the ceiling act as acoustical reflectors. The concert hall is topped by an aluminum-clad volume.

PROJECT TEAM MARIE HOKE, JOHN SMITH, TONY MARTIN, MARK GREEN
MEP ENGINEER E&C ENGINEERS & CONSULTANTS
STRUCTURAL ENGINEER HAYNES WHALEY ASSOCIATES
CIVIL ENGINEER WALTER P. MOORE
IT/DATA CONSULTANT DATACOM DESIGN GROUP
THEATER CONSULTANT SCHULER SHOOK
ACOUSTICAL/AV CONSULTANT JAFFE HOLDEN
COST CONSULTANT PROJECT COST RESOURCES
LANDSCAPE CONSULTANT GARTHOFF DESIGN
ART CONSULTANT ART + ARTISANS
PHOTOGRAPHY AKER IMAGING

www.whrarchitects.com

102,000 sf
10 music rooms
5 theater studios
4 dance studios

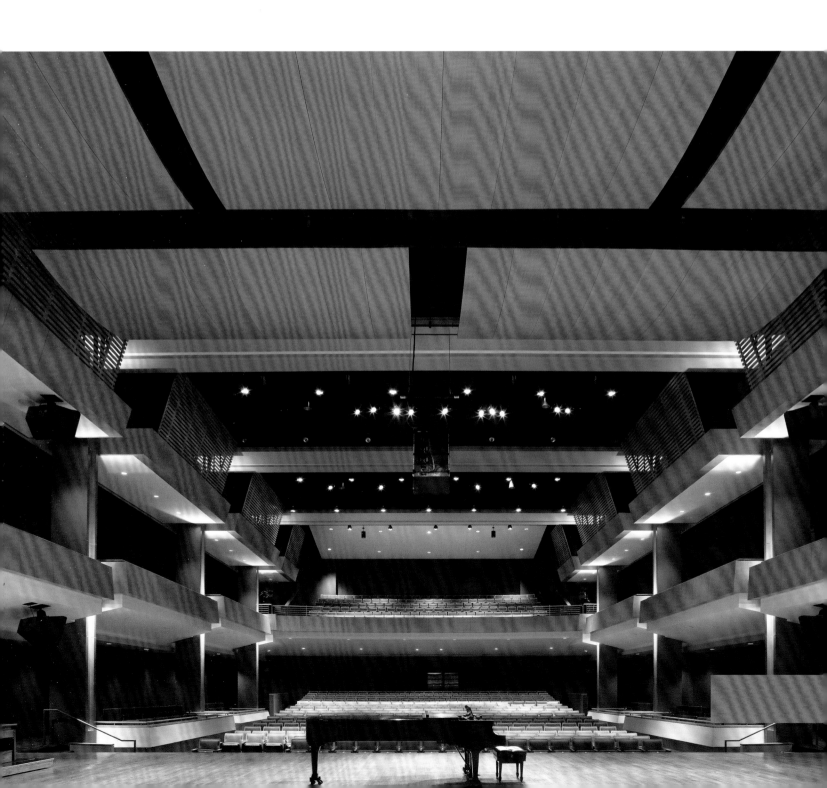

Desai Chia
Architecture

**NEW YORK CHINESE
CULTURAL CENTER, NEW YORK**

As those in the design industry well know, not all worthy projects come to fruition. Such is the case with Desai Chia's reimagined headquarters for NYCCC, a performing arts center for traditional Chinese dance occupying one of Chinatown's quintessentially space-challenged buildings.

To maximize the number of dance studios plus free up room for a reception and seating area—luxuries the center lacked in the snug space—Desai Chia proposed a mezzanine. Steps suspended from the reception ceiling ascend to a balcony office where staff members can work while enjoying views of dancers. The spoke-like latticework surround, rendered in lucky red, takes cues from rice-paper umbrellas and bamboo rings—props used in Chinese dance and acrobatics. The mezzanine is further emboldened by the nonprofit's logo writ large, a signature that works in tandem with the structural system to provide the steel frame with lateral support.

Principals Katherine Chia and Arjun Desai also carved out a warm-up area for students, a move that allows lessons in the main studios to run more efficiently. The glass-enclosed room nestles behind reception, its soaring double-height proportions and floating halo light fixtures creating a theatrical moment almost as thrilling as the Peking Opera and martial-arts performances and workshops taking place in the studio proper.

Clockwise from right:
The steel logo bears the structural load of the mezzanine; reception sits below. The mezzanine is divided by a double-height warm-up studio; a walkway connects the two portions. The warm-up studio. The new floor plan provides the extra facilities needed to allow the cultural center to remain in the heart of Chinatown, accessible to the local community.

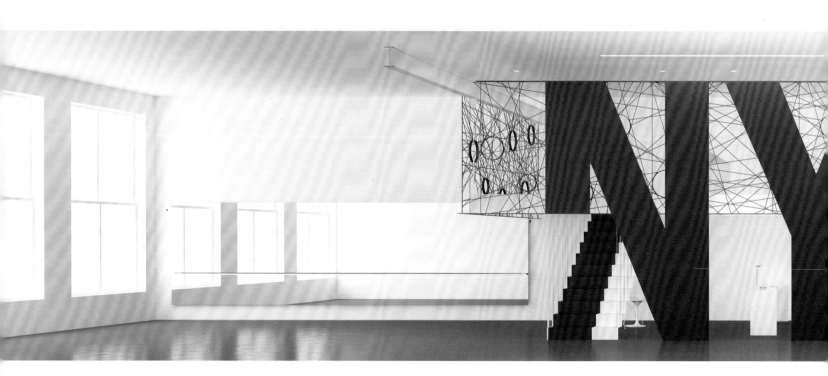

5,000 sf
3 dance studios

PROJECT TEAM KATHERINE CHIA, ARJUN DESAI, HUY DAO
CONSULTANT OLD STRUCTURES
RENDERINGS DESAI CHIA ARCHITECTURE
www.desaichia.com

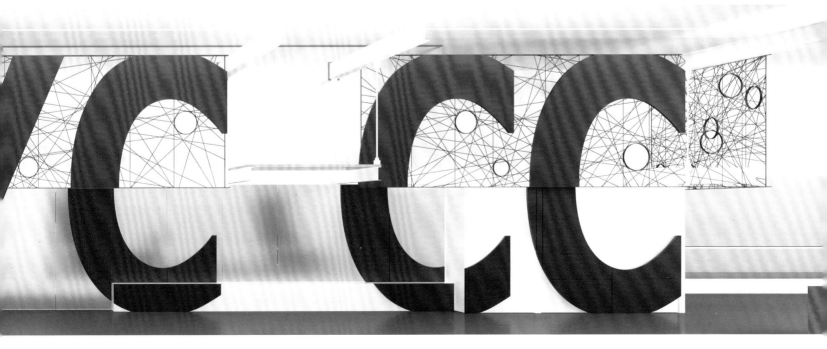

Ennead Architects

THE PUBLIC THEATER, NEW YORK

In the City that Never Sleeps, even landmarks don't stay still. The original stoop of the former Astor Library disappeared long ago, a casualty of street widening. In its place, unceremonious stairs occupied precious lobby space at the 1881 Romanesque Revival edifice, now the Public Theater. Hired to rethink its entry sequence, associate partner Stephen Chu of Ennead Architects (formerly Polshek Partnership) commandeered a loading lane for a new sidewalk and wide black granite steps, sheltered by a glass canopy emblazoned with the theater logo.

Inside, the firm cantilevered an orange-accented mezzanine lounge over the steel-plated box office. At the lobby's center sits a curved resin-coated bar, above which radiates an LED chandelier by Ear Studio. Dubbed the Shakespeare Machine, the signpost-like fixture lights up with lines of dialogue from the Bard's plays (randomly selected by algorithm). Patrons who partake get treated to a quick preview before heading into the theater to see a full production.

The Public Theater's logo is reversed out of the frit-glass canopy. ➤

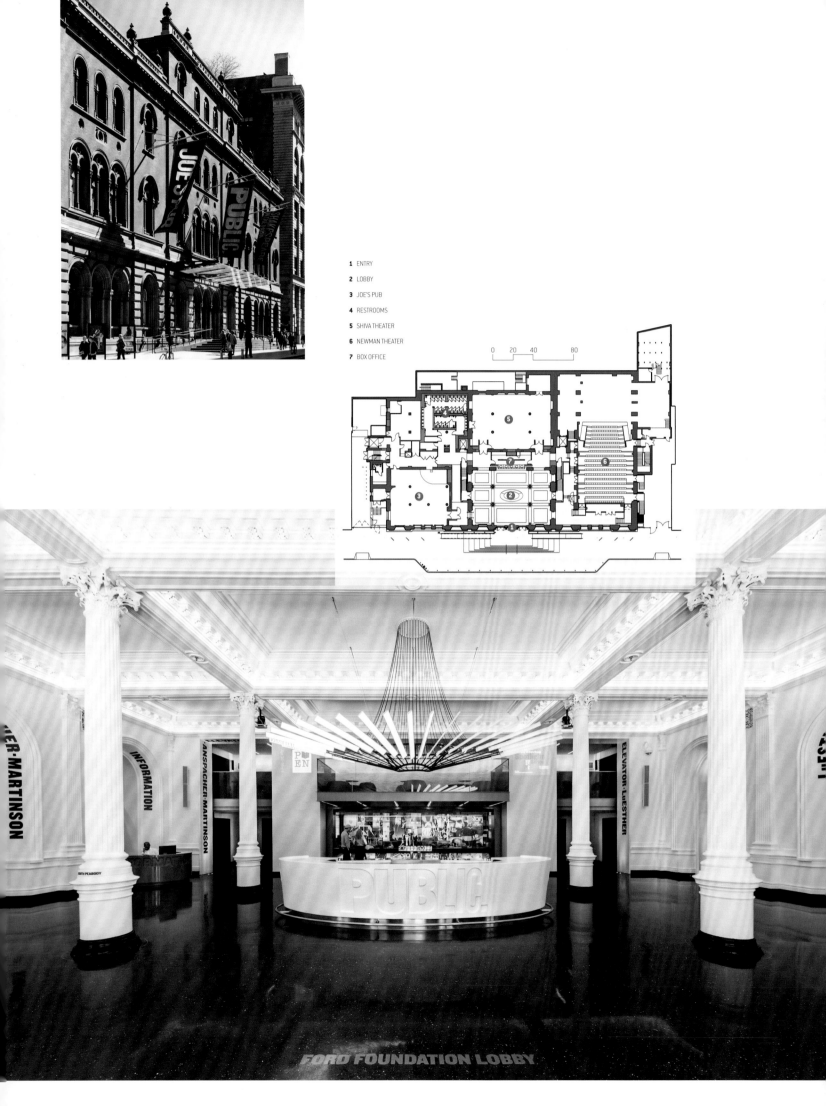

1 ENTRY

2 LOBBY

3 JOE'S PUB

4 RESTROOMS

5 SHIVA THEATER

6 NEWMAN THEATER

7 BOX OFFICE

PROJECT TEAM STEPHEN CHU, DUNCAN HAZARD, JAMES POLSHEK, DAMYANTI RADHESHWAR, KEVIN BAXTER, EDWARD CHRISTIAN, GREGORY SMITH

STRUCTURAL ENGINEER ROBERT SILMAN ASSOCIATES

MEP AMBROSINO, DEPINTO & SCHMIEDER

PRESERVATION BUILDING CONSERVATION ASSOCIATES

LIGHTING CONSULTANT BRANDSTON PARTNERSHIP

GRAPHICS PENTAGRAM

THEATER CONSULTANT AUERBACH, POLLOCK, FRIEDLANDER

ACOUSTICS BENJAMIN HOUGHTON

CIVIL ENGINEER LANGAN ENGINEERING AND ENVIRONMENTAL SERVICES

CONSTRUCTION MANAGER WESTERMAN CONSTRUCTION

PHOTOGRAPHY PETER MAUSS/ESTO (1), JEFF GOLDBERG/ESTO (2–6)

www.ennead.com

Clockwise from right: The new low-profile stoop meshes seamlessly with the landmark brownstone facade. Neoclassical columns contrast with boldfaced wayfinding signage painted on the plaster walls and archways. Pentagram developed the theater's typographic identity. A new steel-and-concrete mezzanine cantilevers over the box office. In the lobby, Ear Studio's light installation displays snippets of Shakespeare on 4-foot-long blades.

Esrawe Studio and Antonio Muñohierro

Clockwise from far left: *Esrawe Studio's renovation included a double-height lobby sheathed in Brazilian teak. The auditorium can hold 1,900 concertgoers. Fiberglass latticework is fitted with acoustic panels that can be backlit with RGB LED strips. Round lighting elements punctuate the gray-painted gypsum walls and ceiling.* ➤

This performing arts center, a six-level complex built in the 1950s, was due a 21st-century rehab. In an ironic twist, its reinvention—completed by multidisciplinary firm Esrawe Studio with an assist from acclaimed film/television designer Antonio Muñohierro—ended up paying tribute to the structure's roots, echoing as it does the evolution of modernism over the decades.

The ground-floor entrance is flanked by art-display niches, one of which occasionally serves as a coat-check area. Backlit circular cutouts in the wall—a retro nod to the building's midcentury roots—are replicated across the double-height lobby ceiling; the planetarium-like vibe gets mirrored in black marble flooring. Teak wainscoting cladding the exterior continues inside, too, wending past mosaic-tile concession counters and into the main concert hall. On both sides of the auditorium is fiberglass latticework fitted with acoustic panels—an artful solution to the challenge of sound management. Among the functional updates is improved lighting, expanded and modernized dressing rooms, and total access for the disabled.

PROJECT TEAM HÉCTOR ESRAWE, ANTONIO MUÑOHIERRO, JOAQUÍN CEVALLOS, NANCY OCAMPO
PHOTOGRAPHY PAÚL RIVERA/ARCHPHOTO

www.esrawe.com

Clockwise from above: *The six-story concert hall has hosted the likes of Rihanna. Circulation pathways are marble. Wainscoting from the exterior carries through to the inside. Another view of the concert hall. Niches in the lobby display sculptures and memorabilia.*

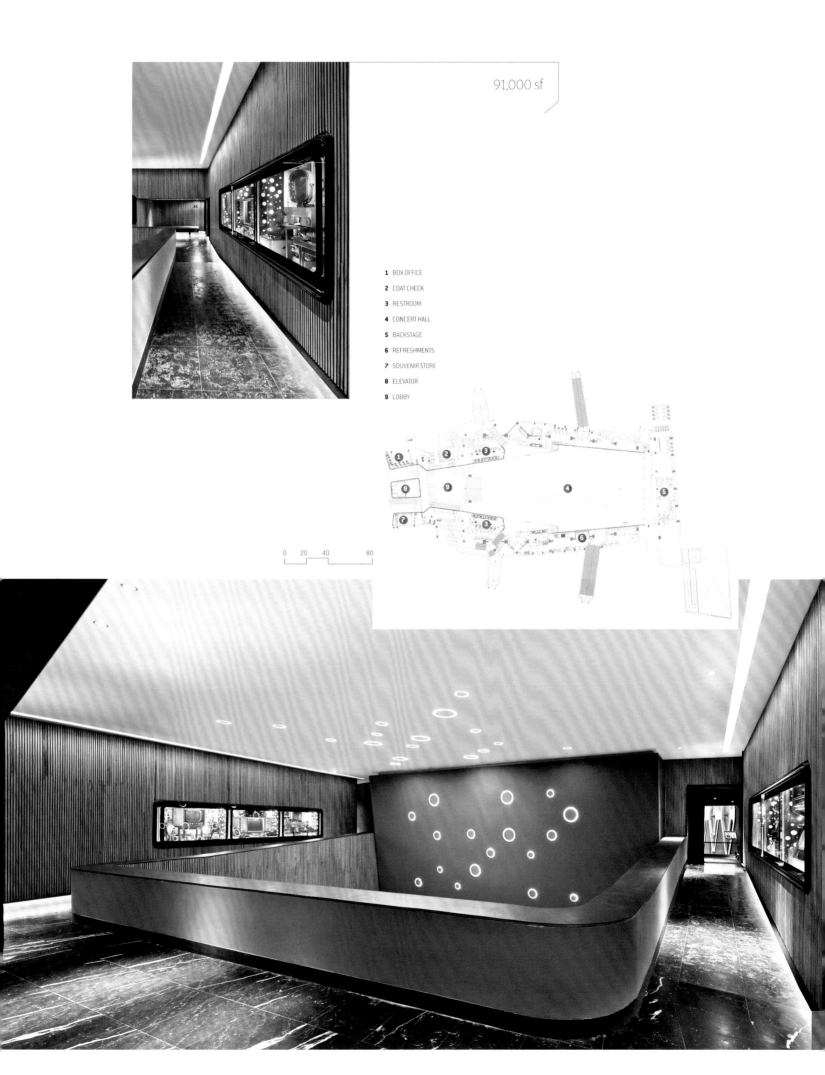

91,000 sf

1 BOX OFFICE

2 COAT CHECK

3 RESTROOM

4 CONCERT HALL

5 BACKSTAGE

6 REFRESHMENTS

7 SOUVENIR STORE

8 ELEVATOR

9 LOBBY

0 20 40 80

H3 Hardy
Collaboration Architecture

LCT3 AT LINCOLN CENTER FOR THE PERFORMING ARTS, NEW YORK

Clockwise from top:
The Claire Tow Theater is located on the roof of the Vivian Beaumont Theater, designed in 1965 by Eero Saarinen & Associates. The addition, contained in a simple rectangular volume, respects the rigor of Saarinen's design. An aluminum screenwall provides shading. ➤

Long before embarking on a decade-long transformation of its 16-acre campus, the Lincoln Center imagined LCT3—a programming initiative devoted to producing new work—as an incubator for the next generation of theater artists. When H3 Hardy Collaboration Architecture was retained to actualize that vision in the form of performance and rehearsal space, firm founder Hugh Hardy surveyed the center's crowded plaza and realized that the only way to go was...up.

Locating the Claire Tow Theater on the roof of the Vivian Beaumont Theater was a bold decision: the latter was designed in 1965 by Eero Saarinen & Associates, one of Hardy's first employers. But the new volume of steel, glass, and aluminum floats discreetly atop the existing structure, supplementing without supplanting. The straightforward

addition was poised on three steel trusses, whose diagonal bracing became a recurring visual element inside and out. By day, the theater subtly appears from just a few vantage points; at night, the new volume seems to hover above the existing roof.

Elevators clad in channel glass open onto the double-height lobby, punctuated by a Kiki Smith sculpture. Visible through floor-to-ceiling glass is an ipe-plank terrace and a green roof featuring eight types of native plants and low-maintenance sedum. In the intimate theater, rich red upholstery gets a warm walnut border. The plan organization wraps the energy-intensive theater with other programming areas, reducing heat gain and loss—and allowing daily-use spaces access to daylight and views.

1   ENTRANCE FOYER

2   BOX OFFICE

3   THEATER

4   DRESSING ROOM

5   REHEARSAL ROOM

6   GREEN ROOM

7   GREEN ROOF

8   TERRACE

9   THEATER LOBBY/CONCESSIONS

0 10 20   40

Clockwise from top: A glass curtain wall and an aluminum screenwall form the building exterior. The airy rehearsal space. The entrance foyer overlooks the terrace though full-height glass. A green roof covers 44 percent of the site footprint. The theater met the need for a more intimate performance space for emerging playwrights. Steel trusses, the longest reaching 150 feet, provide structural bracing.

PROJECT TEAM HUGH HARDY, ARIEL FAUSTO, MERCEDES ARMILLAS,
MARGARET SULLIVAN
PHOTOGRAPHY FRANCIS DZIKOWSKI/OTTO

www.h3hc.com

23,000 sf
112-seat theater
LEED Silver certified
Interior Design 2012 Best of Year
winner, Institutional
AIA New York State Design Award 2013

libraries

As reimagined by a host of innovative thinkers, the contemporary library looks and acts nothing like its staid (if venerable) predecessor.

They are flooded with natural light and animated by daring installation art and zippy graphics. They artfully accommodate both analog and digital media (which can be consumed from the comfort of au courant yet plush seating). And though they nod to the past via familiar touches—wood paneling, full-height stacks—they are just as likely to boast unexpected elements such as a scaled-down Renaissance-style architectural folly or eye-catching light fixtures. As libraries have evolved from reading rooms to community hubs, they now support activities of the not so silent variety, too: Knowledge sharing and chitchat are encouraged. *Talk about turning a new page.*

WEST HOLLYWOOD LIBRARY, LOS ANGELES

Johnson Favaro
and Carol Cambianica

Clockwise from top left: The plywood crate containing the children's theater measures 14 by 20 feet. The theater interior reinvents an Italian Renaissance cityscape. The flooring beyond the circulation desk is clear-finished maple. Limestone plaster clads the building, which is shared with the City Council. ➤

Why build a library today? In the case of this project, that's literally the $64 million question. And the answers are many and multifaceted. "Libraries are the biggest investment a municipality makes," says Johnson Favaro copartner Steve Johnson. The new facility itself is a hive of activity and bold design moves. Also part of a larger picture, it anchors phase one of the firm's master plan for the surrounding West Hollywood Park. By demolishing the former 1960 library and appropriating various parking lots, the architects essentially doubled green space to 7 acres in one of the busiest parts of Los Angeles. So in the center of the community, the design team conceived, well, a community center.

The building was Johnson Favaro's most complicated library-related project yet, as it needed to incorporate City Council offices, too. The Council Chambers and a coffee bar are on the ground level, separated from a bookstore via a porte cochere. Levels two and three belong to the library proper, and tennis courts occupy the roof.

Step inside: pale hues, a neutral scheme by library specialist Carol Cambianica, and commissioned artwork—including a mural by Shepard Fairey—create a gallery-like vibe. Although the library is unquestionably rooted in the present, aspects look to the past. The children's theater, for instance, is housed in a plywood crate, but its interior suggests an Italian Renaissance folly, with a staircase alluding to the one in Michelangelo's Biblioteca Medicea Laurenziana. As with the rest of the facility, the design is anything but bookish.

"We had to choose where to invest resources. The need to gather mechanical functions was also an opportunity to make the canopy a grand gesture, one bigger than the sum of its parts" —JIM FAVARO

In the periodicals section, an elaborately carved bamboo canopy hides HVAC equipment. Under it, leather club chairs and a custom granite-top table gather near rift-cut oak shelving. ⬂

47,500 sf
LEED Gold certified

PROJECT TEAM JIM FAVARO, STEVE JOHNSON, BRIAN DAVIS, MICHAEL SCHULMAN, ERNESTO BARRON, GREG STACKEL, COLE GARRISON, JONATHAN REYES, NATE CHIAPPA, JEFF HABER, ELLEN RIINGEN, BRANDON BLAKEMAN
LIBRARY CONSULTANT LINDA DEMMERS LIBRARY CONSULTING
LIGHTING CONSULTANT LIGHTVISION
ART CONSULTANT MERRY NORRIS CONTEMPORARY ART
SUSTAINABILITY CONSULTANT DAVIS LANGDON
LANDSCAPING CONSULTANT EPT DESIGN
STRUCTURAL ENGINEER ENGLEKIRK STRUCTURAL ENGINEERS
CIVIL ENGINEER KPFF CONSULTING ENGINEERS
MEP M-E ENGINEERS
WOODWORK SMI ARCHITECTURAL MILLWORK
STONEWORK SERENA MARBLE & GRANITE
GENERAL CONTRACTOR W.E. O'NEIL CONSTRUCTION
PHOTOGRAPHY BENNY CHAN/FOTOWORKS

www.johnsonfavaro.com

Clockwise from above:
Bamboo paneling surrounds the stage in the 150-seat Council Chambers. Michelangelo's Biblioteca Medicea Laurenziana in Florence inspired the staircase in the children's theater. The main stairwell features David Weisman's stylized white sycamore, whose leafy branches arch 40 feet overhead. Lining the curtain wall, Lievore Altherr Molina's swivel chairs offer front-row views of the city. The lobby doorway to the Council Chambers is set into a Shepard Fairey mural. The porte cochere is wrapped in Calacatta marble.

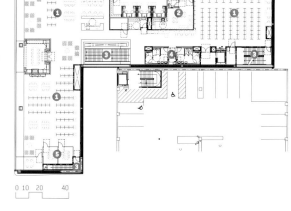

1 READING STACKS
2 STAFF ROOM
3 STAIRCASE
4 RESTROOMS
5 STUDY ROOMS

0 10 20 40

Calvert Wright Architecture | Spatial Discipline

**LEON AND TOBY COOPERMAN LIBRARY
HUNTER COLLEGE, CITY UNIVERSITY OF NEW YORK**

Let's face it—sometimes traditional libraries fall short in meeting contemporary needs. For centuries, they functioned primarily as repositories of received wisdom. But Hunter College's bright-eyed students demanded something different: a dynamic state-of-the-art environment that encouraged, not limited, collaboration. In short, they wanted a space where knowledge could be created, not just stored.

To that end, the university asked principal Calvert Wright to design a variety of activity zones on one floor—the third-floor entry level—of the nine-story library. The project would serve as a trial run, and the most successful areas would be refined and customized in subsequent phases of renovation. A former Princeton and Cornell instructor with ample academic experience, Wright enthusiastically embraced the challenge. "We saw this," he recalls, "as an extraordinary opportunity to design a variety of adaptable spaces so we could focus on the ones that work best and transform the others."

Now there's a study area for every taste: noisy or quiet, collaborative or solitary, social or studious, seated or standing, high-tech or low-tech, traditional or casual. The café busts conventions as well. Students had requested spaces where long-standing restrictions on food and noise would be relaxed so they could study, nosh, and socialize at once. Wright's team obliged with diner-style booths featuring whiteboard-top tables for impromptu meetings. And how popular are they? The demand is so great, students must make reservations.

17,500 sf
3rd-floor renovation
LEED Gold registered

Clockwise from top:
Tufted resilient sheet flooring provides some of the acoustic benefits of carpeting—with added durability and stain resistance. Near the entrance, sawtooth wall cabinets exhibit items from the library's special collections. An LED "ticker tape" in the stairwell scrolls through donor names; the surrounding walls are painted in a gradient of the school color. The suspended ceiling, made of perforated and corrugated steel panels, is lit from above to cast a soft glow on the floor. ➤

PROJECT TEAM CALVERT WRIGHT, AIA; CHRIS HEINTZEN, RA, LEED AP; FABIAN BEDOLLA; ALEX WITKO
CONSULTANT PRICE ASHER GROUP
MEP ENGINEER KAM CHIU ASSOCIATES
PHOTOGRAPHY BJÖRG MAGNEA
www.spatialdiscipline.com

Gilder Tirschwell Information Commons

WELCOME TO THE GILDER TIRSCHWELL INFORMATION COMMONS

Bershad
reference desk

Bershad Reference Desk
Leon and Toby Cooperman Library

REFERENCE

1 ENTRY

2 WELCOME DESK

3 ELEVATOR BANK

4 DIGITAL DINER/CAFÉ

5 READING AREA

6 INFORMATION COMMONS

7 REFERENCE DESK

0 10 20   40

Clockwise from top:
*Digital signage behind
the reference desk
broadcasts college
news, events, and
tweets. Backlit glass
wall panels double as
whiteboards in the
reading area.
Wayfinding elements
are based on the
1970s Massimo
Vignelli New York City
subway-map design.
Archival images from
the library are
replicated on room
signs. The idea of
topping custom
café tables with white-
board laminate was
sparked by the
practice of students
carving their initials
into wooden desktops.*

Álvarez-Díaz & Villalón

SAINT JOHN'S SCHOOL LIBRARY
SAN JUAN, PUERTO RICO

Clockwise from opposite: In the periodicals nook and throughout, durable nylon carpet tile from Milliken features a pattern of abstracted book spines (and is appropriately named Stacks). Glass-enclosed reading rooms offer quiet space for study. Steelcase ottomans are mobile, encouraging collaboration and a relaxed work environment. ➤

Over the past decade, Álvarez-Díaz & Villalón has stayed ahead of the curve, forging an international reputation for environmentally responsible design. The firm's motto? "Sustainable practice is a global movement and each of us needs to play our part," say founders Ricardo Álvarez-Díaz and Cristina Villalón.

That stance guided their renovation of a prep-school library connecting a pair of century-old buildings—a two-story middle school and a three-story high school. Eco-savvy elements conserve energy and lower operating costs, reducing the carbon footprint: VOC-free paints and adhesives, sensor-controlled LED lighting that emits 100 lumens while consuming just 32 watts, ceiling tiles boasting 71 percent recycled material, NSF- and Smart-certified carpet tile with PVC-free backing. The design is not only green but it's also, well, green, with accents specified in Saint John's school color. Lime tones pop up strategically in flooring and furnishings, leavening an otherwise muted palette of gray textiles and oak-laminate millwork.

The previously dark, cluttered space is now primarily open-plan, with varied zones to accommodate a range of study styles—from lounge and table seating to an enclosed quiet area. Legible modern signage and state-of-the-art AV and computer technology (touch-screen PCs, wireless printing) uphold the contemporary look.

The firm's greatest accomplishment, though, may well be its grace under fire. Given just eight weeks—the school's summer break—from demo to completion, the architects had to grapple with a number of structural surprises, including peculiarly angled perimeter walls and floors that didn't align. They met the strict deadline thanks to fast footwork and creative problem solving on-site, honed through years of experience.

current periodicals

5,440 sf
12,000 volumes

PROJECT TEAM RICARDO ÁLVAREZ-DÍAZ, AIA; CRISTINA VILLALÓN, CODDI; GILBERTO IBARRA, AIA, LEED AP; ESTEFANIA ALEJANDRO, AAIA; JOAQUIN HERNANDEZ
HVAC CONSULTANT JORGE LEDON WEBSTER
ELECTRICAL CONSULTANT REQUENA AND ASSOCIATES
PHOTOGRAPHY CARLOS PÉREZ LÓPEZ

www.alvarezdiazvillalon.com

0   10   20   40

1 HIGH SCHOOL ENTRANCE
2 LIBRARY SHELVING
3 QUIET STUDY ROOM
4 CIRCULATION DESK
5 MEDIA CENTER
6 MIDDLE SCHOOL ENTRANCE
7 MEETING ROOM
8 READING AREA

Clockwise from right:
A concealed partition allows the media area to be closed off. Chairs are upholstered in Cradle to Cradle–certified polyester. Above the circulation desk, signage with 8-inch-high sans serif lettering is easy to read—and makes a modern statement. The long, narrow volume features the main area's group-study zones and steel bookshelves at the center, with a media room on one side and perimeter rooms for quiet study on the other.

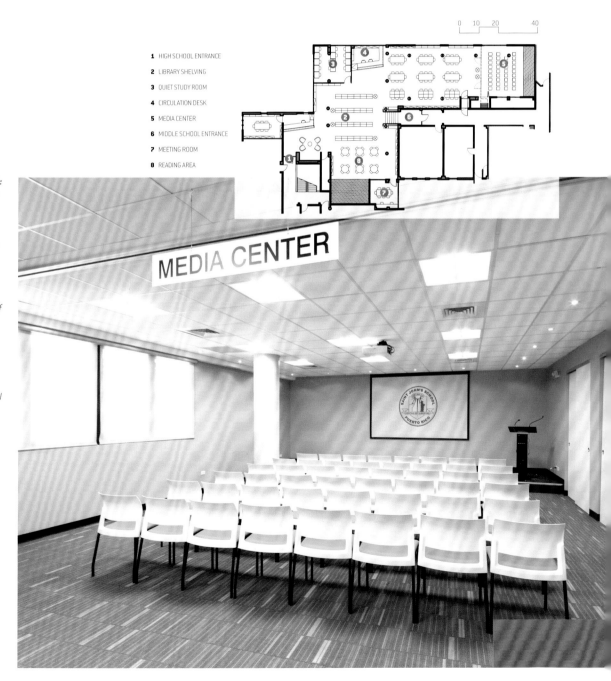

Vermilion Zhou Design Group

SHANGHAI JIADING PUBLIC LIBRARY AND CULTURAL CENTER

Principal Ray Zhou's first child was born during this library project, perhaps explaining the heart put into the kid-friendly touches in the youth section. Whimsy abounds, from the birch birdcage-shape pendant fixtures and chair sizes for various ages to the playground nestled amid circulation shelving. It's especially present in the round structural columns, where abstracted branches sprout as if from tree trunks, creating the sense one is wandering through an enchanted forest. Furthering the woodsy theme is the natural timber used throughout for desktops, the canopy, and more. "The design concept derives from Jiangnan, a classic southern Chinese building style typified by a wooden structure capped with a pitched roof," explains Zhou. "That sparked the emphasis on the interior ceilings."

Zhou prioritized views and light, both of which receive special attention in traditional courtyard architecture. The building forms a U around a reflecting pool, which is crossed via stepping-stones at ground level and, on the second story, by a glass-wall bridge housing a computer room. (It leads to the cultural center boasting a 500-seat theater.) The gray-brick exterior is urban, even sober. But like the unassuming door to Narnia, it hides a wonderland.

Clockwise from left: Custom computer-station tables furnish the children's area. Neutral woven-vinyl flooring complements pale Scandinavian-style timber in the children's reading room. The general reading room's wood-laminate magazine stands. ➤

280,000 sf

"The design of the public spaces reflects the new minimalist Chinese philosophy" —RAY ZHOU

Clockwise from opposite: Powder-coated-steel pendants hang in the general literature reading room. The main stacks. The electronic reading room features a smoked-oak canopy with LED-lit cutouts. ➤

Clockwise from above: The theater at the cultural center seats 500. Stair treads are made of marble. The building forms a horseshoe around a reflecting pool, which is spanned by a glass-wall bridge. George Nelson pendants illuminate the special collections reading room. Twin entrances in the lobby lead to the theater.

1 ENTRY PLAZA

2 24-HOUR LIBRARY

3 THEATER

4 MULTI-FUNCTION ROOM

5 PATIO

6 ART ROOM

7 GENERAL LIBRARY

8 CHILDREN'S READING AREA

9 ELECTRONIC READING ROOM

10 BOOK CLUB AND CAFÉ

11 FRONT DESK

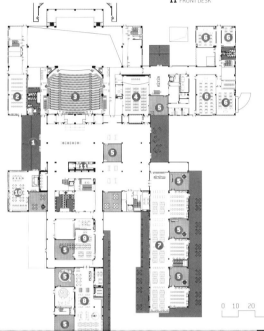

0 10 20   40

PROJECT TEAM RAY ZHOU, VERA CHU, GARVIN HUNG, ZHAO JUN HE
PHOTOGRAPHY DERRYCK MENERE

www.vermilionzhou.com

2,664 sf
$80 per sf budget

Befitting a school run by Catholic Sisters, this library in Guatemala City's Zone 13 is simple, austere, and honest, reflecting an architecture where—as firm partner Mauricio Solis puts it—"nothing is superfluous." The facade's locally sourced earthenware bricks, called *fachaleta*, vary in hue according to the length of kiln time, yielding a subtle but chromatically rich canvas.

The three-level project, funded entirely by the Korean International Cooperation Agency, encompasses a triple-height lobby, auditorium, computer lab, and reading room, rendered in a restrained palette of exposed concrete, perforated PVC paneling, zebrawood, and recycled OSB. The conceptual heart of the project is the second-floor green roof, accessed via a bridge from the library. There the students—mainly girls from low-income households—can lounge alfresco on grassy manmade knolls. The indoor reading room soars two stories to lend appropriate grandeur to this place of literature and learning—and dignity to the young and vulnerable population it houses.

SolisColomer y Asociados Arquitectos

KOICA LIBRARY, VILLA DE LAS NIÑAS, GUATEMALA CITY

Clockwise from above: Skylights invite natural illumination into the reading room, where Ross Lovegrove's Supernatural chairs add a touch of color. Zebrawood paneling defines the stairway and landing. Desks accented with yellow Formica panels animate the computer lab. A black-painted concrete footbridge connects the green roof to the neighboring school building. The new library occupies a small site between two existing structures. The student body congregates in the auditorium, where the glazed earthenware tiles of the exterior walls reappear.

PROJECT TEAM MAURICIO SOLIS, CARLOS VALLADARES, ROBERTO MELGAR, EDDY LÓPEZ
CONSTRUCTION CC GRUPO
WOODWORK INSTALLATION MUEBLES MADEIRA
CONCRETE AND GLAZED BRICKS INMACO
PHOTOGRAPHY BYRON MÁRMOL
www.soliscolomer.com

Calvert Wright
Architecture | Spatial Discipline

ZABAR ART LIBRARY AND SCREENING
ROOM, HUNTER COLLEGE
CITY UNIVERSITY OF NEW YORK

The primary goal of this project was to create a shared facility for students and faculty from three departments: Art, Art History, and Film & Media. The program called for learning, screening, and exhibition space that could accommodate both group and solo work, as well as physical and digital collections. As if that wasn't already a lot to resolve, Calvert Wright also had to reconcile divergent design visions. Some stakeholders wanted a very modern aesthetic; others suggested a more time-honored look. To please both parties, Wright proposed as the primary material quarter-sawn white oak with a clear finish. The modernists appreciated the natural finish and clean, unornamented detailing. (Indeed, the art faculty was quick to point out that MoMA uses the same cut and species of wood for its floors.) To the traditionalists, white oak suggested Stickley furniture and the iconic Reading Room tables of the flagship New York Public Library.

Speaking of furnishings, classicists requested old-school tables and chairs, while progressive voices lobbied for casual seating and collaborative spaces. So to abet group work, Wright designed traditional tables—though wired for power, with double-wide tops—and seating with casters.

Although every new academic facility requires ultra up-to-date technology, no one wanted gadgetry to overwhelm the space. Wright devised a number of fixes to hide such elements. One of his most inspired moves was integrating the screening room's speakers and projector into the fabric-wrapped acoustic ceiling panels. Who says you can't please everyone?

7,250 sf

PROJECT TEAM CALVERT WRIGHT, AIA; CHRIS HEINTZEN, RA, LEED, AP;
FABIAN BEDOLLA, RA
CONSULTANT PRICE ASHER GROUP
PHOTOGRAPHY BJÖRG MAGNEA

www.spatialdiscipline.com

Clockwise from bottom: Loaner laptops used in lieu of monitors keep the white-oak study tables uncluttered. The screening room doubles as a traditional classroom for students in the Art, Art History, and Film & Media departments. Window seats in the form of upholstered banquettes take advantage of natural light and views. Instead of placing wall outlets around the screening room, Calvert Wright integrated power sources into the base of each seat. Vibrant seating accents the bright, airy space.

To transform a mundane library at Archbishop Molloy High School into a multifunctional, technology-based facility in tune with the 21st century, Tobin Parnes Design employed simplicity and practicality at every turn. Principals Robert Parnes, Carol Tobin, and Gerard Orozco channeled classic traditionalism in conceiving a space that would nod to the grand timber-lined libraries of the 19th century.

The rectangular footprint is flanked by windows on one side; opposite them are library shelves whose shifting contours form study alcoves. The cherry-hued veneer and laminate that recurs throughout—on table legs, bookcases, and ceiling elements—unifies the space while carpet tile helps delineate zones. Green measures also abound: There are solar shades that invite natural light in while reducing glare, energy-efficient LED fluorescents, low-VOC paints, rooms with individual thermostats, and original bookshelves repurposed as side tables.

A computer lab, conference room, dedicated college-prep workstations, and space suitable for large events and everyday study were the client's main requirements. The school was also intent on including a curved component... but where? An arched ceiling—proposed by Tobin Parnes—was an idea the school hadn't considered, but the end result earned the highest of praise.

PROJECT TEAM CAROL TOBIN, ROBERT PARNES, GERARD OROZCO, GORDON T. LAPLANTE, ANDREA DIBNER, ELFI MELO, CHELSEA WATLINGTON
PHOTOGRAPHY VANNI ARCHIVE
www.tobinparnes.com

Clockwise from right: *Existing wood bookcase built-ins were stripped and stained to match the color of the new laminate. In the conference room, bronze lantern-style pendants with tinted, frosted glass cast a soft glow. The arches were made with painted plasterboard and cherrywood plastic-laminate inserts. Upholstered seating furnishes the lounge area.*

Tobin Parnes Design

WILLIAM J. MURPHY LIBRARY, ARCHBISHOP MOLLOY HIGH SCHOOL, QUEENS, NEW YORK

3,200 sf
Built during
summer recess

youth

Tots, teens, and all ages in between need creative yet functional spaces in which to learn and play. Designers are rising to that challenge, thinking outside the (toy)box and eschewing the expected primary colors in favor of thoughtful concepts big on whimsy, fun, and high design. From preschools and summer camps to outdoor-activity pavilions and communal gardens, all give youths a feeling of agency. What's in: facilities for scientific experiment, indoor tree houses, and getting kids outside and in touch with nature. *Here's to never growing up.*

4,400 sf
Interior Design Best of Year 2012
Award, Institutional Youth
AIA Central States Region
2012 Architectural Honor Award

Serving the Girl Scouts of Northeast Kansas and Northwest Missouri, Camp Prairie Schooner sits on 176 wooded acres of creeks, hills, and hiking trails high on the bluffs of the Little Blue River. El Dorado principal Douglas Stockman contributed a 4,400-square-foot trail center consisting of adjoining bunkhouses—each with a lounge, kitchen, and sleep and shower areas for 20 campers and four counselors—along with common restrooms.

Fabricated of corrugated steel and translucent polycarbonate, the structures feature low-maintenance concrete floors. Furnishings include Eric Pfeiffer stools and custom bunk beds in powdercoated steel and painted birch plywood, made by Stockman's architecture students at Kansas State University. Pendant fixtures found on Etsy were handcrafted by California lighting designer Brandi Pulver, once a Scout herself. The exterior cement-board siding is rendered in tangerine, lime, and plum, a palette inspired by the colorful packaging of Do-si-dos, Thin Mints, and Samoas.

Clockwise from top:
Cement-board siding comes in playful hues. Custom bunk beds were made by the architect's Kansas State University students. Bed frames are powdercoated steel and painted birch plywood. El Dorado's connecting bunkhouses joined the preexisting dining hall, located nearby.

El Dorado

CAMP PRAIRIE SCHOONER
KANSAS CITY, MISSOURI

1 RESTROOMS

2 BUNKROOM

3 COUNSELOR ROOM

4 KITCHEN

5 FLEXIBLE SPACE

0   10   20   40

Clockwise from right:
Eric Pfeiffer stools in durable polyethylene make a jaunty statement in the kitchen. Flooring throughout is simple concrete. The cheerful exterior can be downlit come dusk. Corrugated steel composes the majority of the facade. Skylights punctuate bunkhouse roofs.

PROJECT TEAM DOUGLAS STOCKMAN, SEAN SLATTERY, BRANDON FROELICH
PHOTOGRAPHY MIKE SINCLAIR

www.eldo.us

WorkAC

P.S. 216 EDIBLE SCHOOLYARD, BROOKLYN, NEW YORK

Clockwise from top: The Edible School-yard's exterior features painted cement shingles and steel-rimmed porthole windows. Aluminum-framed polycarbonate panels enclose the greenhouse. A fir pergola shelters outdoor classes. ➤

California chef Alice Waters established her first Edible Schoolyard in 1995 so that Berkeley children could cook and eat fresh produce cultivated in gardening classes. Now New York's first Edible Schoolyard has taken root, supplanting a half acre of asphalt at Public School 216 Arturo Toscanini in the Gravesend neighborhood of Brooklyn. WorkAC principal Amale Andraos and her husband, fellow principal Dan Wood, got the job after receiving raves for a farm-inspired installation commissioned by MoMA PS1 for its annual summertime Young Architects Program.

Part of the site is a thriving organic garden. In the center stands a structure with two main teaching components: a kitchen and a greenhouse. The choice of translucent polycarbonate panels to enclose the latter "was a cost decision," Wood explains. "But we liked the blurring effect." Cheerful porthole windows punctuate the kitchen's jaunty facade, clad in inexpensive fish-scale cement shingles painted to form stylized blooms. The graphic exterior is an homage to the floral facade of Venturi, Scott Brown and Associates's iconic 1978 Best Products Catalog showroom in Pennsylvania. Inside the kitchen, the same color palette enlivens cabinets. Adjacent, a brilliant blue volume houses sustainable features such as a cistern for rainwater. The sprightly hue, Woods says, imbues mundane technology with the wonder of a giant toy.

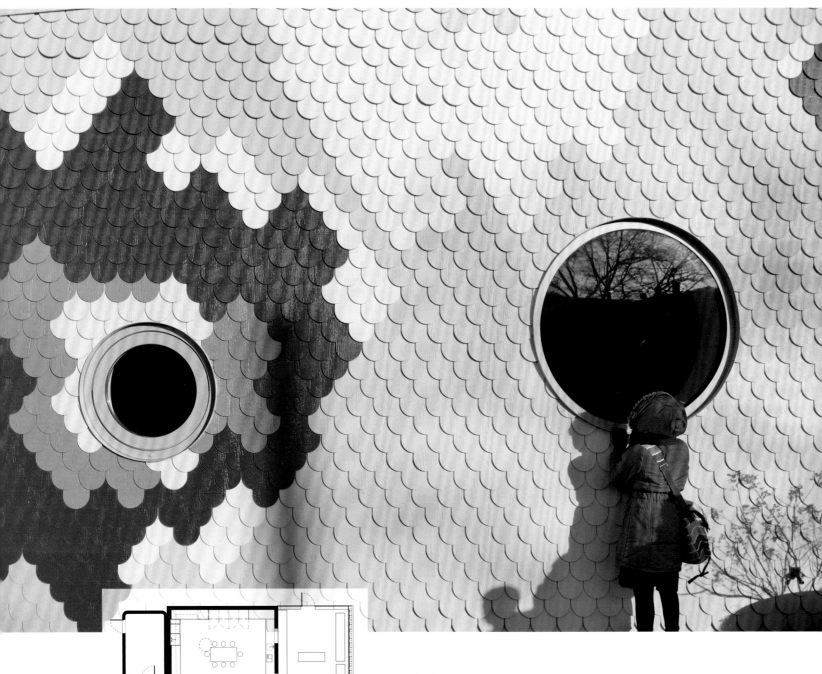

Clockwise from above: The colorful fish-scale facade. Lacquered MDF fronts cabinets in the teaching kitchen. Elementary school students learn how to grow their own vegetables in the greenhouse. The blue rubber-sprayed structure houses a rainwater cistern and an energy-efficient air-conditioning unit.

0   5   10   20

1 SYSTEMS WALL

2 KITCHEN CLASSROOM

3 GREENHOUSE

4 OFFICE

5 RESTROOM

2,300 sf

PROJECT TEAM AMALE ANDRAOS, DAN WOOD, MICHAEL BLANCATO, JASON ANDERSON, METTE BLANKENBERG, DINA BRAENDSTRUP, TOBIAS HERR, ANNA KENOFF, CYRIL MARSOLLIER, ANNE MENKE, JESUNG PARK, MIKE ROBITZ, SAM DUFAUX, MAGGIE TSANG
ARCHITECT OF RECORD PERKINS EASTMAN
STRUCTURAL ENGINEER LESLIE E. ROBERTSON ASSOCIATES
MEP PLUS GROUP
CIVIL ENGINEER SHERWOOD DESIGN ENGINEERS
LIGHTING DESIGN TILLOTSON DESIGN ASSOCIATES
GENERAL CONTRACTOR NESCO
PHOTOGRAPHY IWAN BAAN

www.work.ac

NYRP EDGE/UCATION PAVILION
AND BOATHOUSE, NEW YORK

Desai Chia
Architecture

In Hurricane Sandy's wake, the ecologically minded New York Restoration Project launched a design competition to ensure the future of Sherman Creek Park. Why? Its Inwood location—in a flood zone on the banks of the tidal Harlem River—makes it particularly vulnerable to inclement weather. Desai Chia Architecture was selected as a finalist for its concept, which encompasses two community pavilions—a boathouse and a classroom—linked by a boardwalk that doubles as an activity area. The design allows extreme tidal surges of the kind Sandy produced to simply flow under the structures and around piles of timber, a material chosen for its salt-resistant property.

The boathouse, with space for 24 kayaks, is capped with a roof of prefabricated corrugated-aluminum panels that are set at gentle angles to direct rainwater runoff into giant cisterns. Wire-mesh walls are at once porous and secure. Between the pavilions lies a reclaimed-pine boardwalk dotted with benches and tables, planters, and racks that can be used to dry damp clothes or as trellises for greenery to climb. In the adjacent education hut, wooden bleachers and lockable storage units provide an alfresco yet sheltered setting for science experiments. Here, steps descend to marshland, one of six precious ecological habitats that kids—and curious adults—are encouraged to explore.

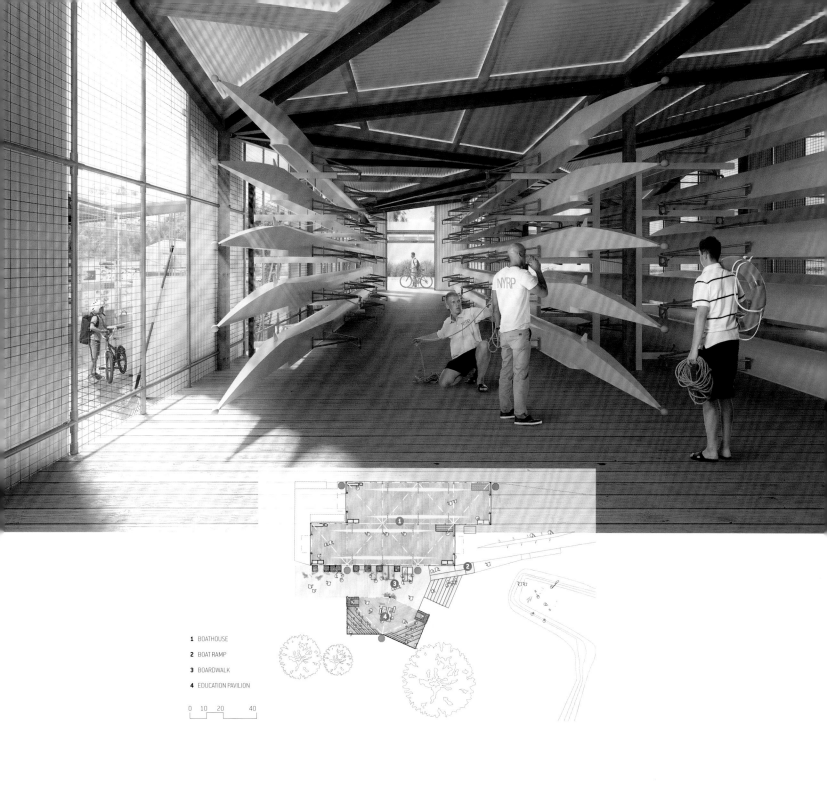

1 BOATHOUSE

2 BOAT RAMP

3 BOARDWALK

4 EDUCATION PAVILION

0   10   20   40

Clockwise from left:
Desai Chia's buildings
are designed to sit as
lightly as possible on
the terrain, allowing
the unique habitats at
the water's edge to
thrive. Rainwater
collected from the roof
of the boathouse can
be used to wash down
the kayaks within.
The reclaimed-pine
boardwalk, set
between the two pavil-
ions, leads to a boat
dock. The boardwalk
also accommodates
outdoor activities.

10,000 sf
Net-zero project

PROJECT TEAM KATHERINE CHIA, ARJUN DESAI, HUY DAO, KENNETH MITCHELL
STRUCTURAL ENGINEER CONSULTANT ARUP
CIVIL ENGINEER CONSULTANT MUESER RUTLEDGE CONSULTING ENGINEERS
ECOLOGY CONSULTANT RAFT LANDSCAPE
RENDERINGS AVOID OBVIOUS, DESAI CHIA ARCHITECTURE

www.desaichia.com

Although the entire country suffered during the three-decade-long civil war ending in 1996, the Ixil Triangle—a trio of isolated towns in the Western Highlands—was especially hard hit in the early 1980s. The Guatemalan military decimated the area's predominantly Ixil population in an effort to thwart guerilla activity, and the towns were literally erased from official maps for the duration.

Replacing lost infrastructure is now a high priority, and that's where SolisColomer y Asociados Arquitectos came in. With the project aided by a grant from the International Cooperation Agency of Korea, the local architecture firm envisioned seven elementary schools with the budget in mind—and clearly didn't skimp on high design.

At one of the schools, San Felipe Chenla, swooping pavilions connect to a row of classrooms rendered in raw concrete. Ceramic-tile parapets spiral around stairs and wrap decks—including a rooftop terrace—that echo the topography of the surrounding Cuchumatanes: the highest nonvolcanic mountain range in Central America.

For the brightly stained pine sliding doors that animate two sides of the rectangular classroom block, the architects referenced the local Ixil culture, taking inspiration from the traditional handwoven, often embroidered tunics called *huipils*. Further chromatic pop was added via orange polyethylene chairs for students and sunny yellow podiums for teachers.

SolisColomer y Asociados Arquitectos

ESCUELA SAN FELIPE CHENLA
QUICHÉ, GUATEMALA

Clockwise from below: Some 240 pupils attend San Felipe Chenla elementary school. The pine sliding doors enclosing classrooms were treated to a turquoise stain. Patterns on the metal shutters nod to huipil, the indigenous central Mexican and Central American garment whose design and color varies by region. Black tiles cladding a balcony parapet continue down the sides of a curved staircase. Colorful classroom furniture enlivens floors of white porcelain tile.

PROJECT TEAM MAURICIO SOLÍS, ROBERTO MELGAR, EDDY LÓPEZ, JOSE JORGE NAVAS, RALPHY GALICIA, JULIO VALDÉS, FRANCISCO VELÁZQUEZ, GUSTAVO LIMA, BILLY JACOBS, HECTOR PÉREZ, HUGO PÉREZ
PHOTOGRAPHY MARIANO VADILLO (1, 3, 4), MARKO BRADICH (2, 5)

soliscolomer.com

9,700 sf

Adults encourage children to learn, but kids just want to have fun. Preschool is where those two goals intertwine, as Joey Ho demonstrated with a fanciful but modern instructional space where good-natured imagination reigns.

The palette is fresh, almost Scandinavian, mixing powder blue, chartreuse, and white with clear-finished blond wood. Many elements bring kids into dialogue with the world of grown-ups. For example, fountainlike dual-height washbasins allow everyone to use the same restrooms, and cooking lessons take place in a professional-style stainless-steel kitchen, scaled down for small statures. If tots need to speak to the staff member behind the reception desk, a short staircase brings them up to eye level.

Playful details abound. There are ceiling-mount swings, cozy reading pods, and an airy gymnasium for romping. The whimsical centerpiece of the lunchroom is a structural column serving as a tree and supporting a mezzanine "tree house." When the teacher announces it's time to come back down, youngsters can just take the slide.

SPRING LEARNING CENTER, HONG KONG

Joey Ho Design

Clockwise from near right: Mounted on the reception ceiling, above the desk and mini staircase, is the school name—with its illuminated "n," a mathematics symbol for infinity, dangling. Wall graphics take advantage of doorway shapes to mimic a city skyline. A slide descends from a loft-level playroom known as the tree house. Among the seating options are kid-size Eames chairs. ➘

1 ACTIVITY ROOMS

2 RESTROOM

3 KITCHEN

4 CAFÉ

5 TREE HOUSE

6 MEETING ROOMS

7 STAFF ROOM

8 GYMNASIUM

9 RECEPTION

0   10   20   40

Clockwise from top:
In the café, "pods" serve
as comfy cocoons for
kids to read or surf the
Web in. The dual-height
washbasin in the
restroom works for
children and adults
alike. Kitchen counters
and equipment are sized
down. Basketball court
markings on the
gymnasium ceiling were
created with LEDs.

PROJECT TEAM JOEY HO, NOEL CHAN
PHOTOGRAPHY DICK LIU
www.joeyhodesign.com

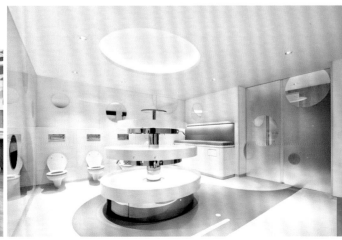

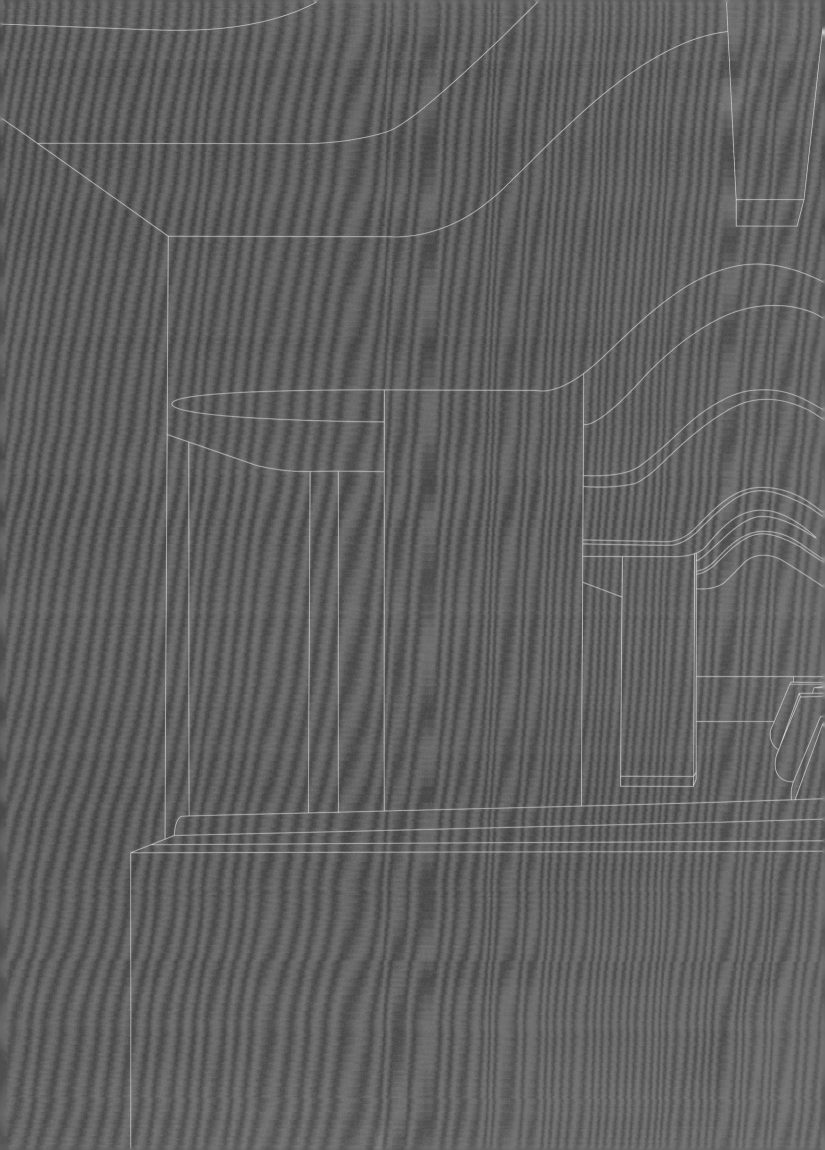

higher education

Lively, wired, and future-ready, these learning environments were conceived to excite and inspire. The firms behind them definitely did their homework, creating spaces tailored to end users. One polled students to determine the ergonomics of their study habits; another analyzed market trends in undergrad housing. Many designers harnessed sustainable strategies, recycling surplus energy, democratically distributing light, and embracing adaptive reuse. Every available square inch—and quirk—is put to practical purpose, whether the project in question is a dreary office complex reinvented as vibrant student housing or a forward-thinking study hub occupying the idle space under a historic sports stadium. *Best in class, indeed.*

Perkins+Will Canada

TRENT COMMUNITY SPORT AND RECREATION CENTER, PETERBOROUGH, ONTARIO

Overlooking the Otonabee River, this dynamic athletic facility is the by-product of a seamless integration of old and new construction. Trent University tapped Perkins+Will Canada to graft a two-story addition—a composition of copper, polished architectural block, and glass—to its existing athletic building at the south end of campus. The tip-to-toe revamp includes a SwimEx hydrotherapy pool, an expanded therapy clinic, updated and redesigned changing rooms, and a Wi-Fi-equipped café. A unique feature is the innovative indoor rowing and paddling tank, the most advanced of its kind in North America—and an officially sanctioned Olympic training ground.

Sustainability drove the design, with LEED Silver certification as the target. To that end, myriad eco-conscious strategies were employed: heat recovery on air and water systems, daylight harvesting, energy-efficient lighting, water-efficient plumbing fixtures, drought-tolerant indigenous planting, locally sourced recycled materials, and the adaptive reuse of an existing structure.

Another aim was to better engage both the student body and the community at large. The expanded and modernized facility has already paid dividends, attracting more members and a wider demographic—and providing a model for other university athletic departments aspiring to similar goals.

80,000 sf
$14.15 million project cost
LEED Silver certified

Clockwise from top left: The low-profile exterior stays out of competition with the natural environment. A state-of-the-art climbing wall creates a dynamic point of interest in the weight room. The custom rowing tank was designed in collaboration with the university's rowing club, a local yacht designer, and a manufacturer of stainless-steel pools. ➤

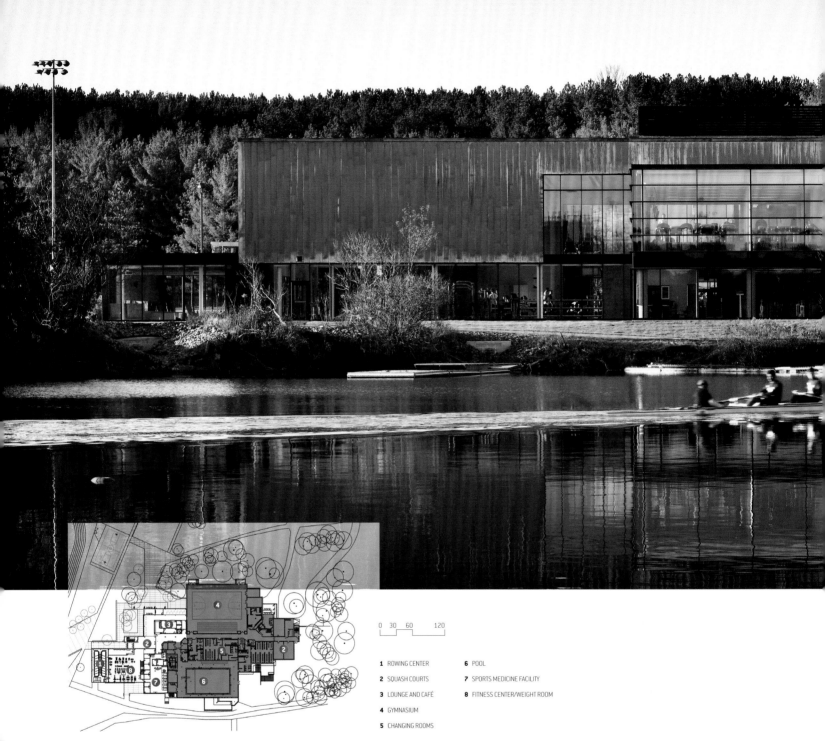

0 30 60   120

1 ROWING CENTER   **6** POOL

2 SQUASH COURTS   **7** SPORTS MEDICINE FACILITY

3 LOUNGE AND CAFÉ   **8** FITNESS CENTER/WEIGHT ROOM

4 GYMNASIUM

5 CHANGING ROOMS

PROJECT TEAM D'ARCY ARTHURS, PHIL FENECH, DUFF BALMER, ALAN MORTSCH,
LIZ LIVINGSTON, MIKE SALIJ, GAVIN GUTHRIE, GREGORY BECK RUBIN, HEATH
CHURCHILL, PERRY EDWARDS, STEPHANIE WETMORE
PHOTOGRAPHY TOM ARBAN

www.perkinswill.ca

Clockwise from top:
*Copper siding clads
the new building.
Newly constructed
and renovated spaces
were gracefully
combined. In the
dramatic double-
height lobby, a "box"
clad in wood phenolic
panels housing the
reception and café
acts as the new
greeting point of the
facility. Strategic
glazing in the
12,000-square-foot
weight room invites
views of the Otonabee
River.*

Hickok Cole
Architects

CONSTANCE MILSTEIN AND FAMILY
ACADEMIC CENTER, NEW YORK UNIVERSITY
WASHINGTON, D.C.

Clockwise from above: *In a lecture theater, custom wood-veneer walls with block cutouts are lined with acoustical treatment. A 13-by-45-foot map of the city spans one lobby wall; New York Avenue is highlighted in the school color. Linear gestures embellish walls and floors, heightening the impression of expansiveness. The facade's statement-making glass fins clad the dormitory levels.* ➤

Hickok Cole Architects was tapped to design New York University's Global Academic Center in Washington, D.C., one of several Network Centers worldwide. Seeking to distinguish itself architecturally from other semester programs in the nation's capital, the client encouraged the firm to design something unique and progressive. The building achieves this aspiration while expressing the functional elements of the program, tucked into a compact infill site.

The solid stone base envelops the first and second floors, which contain public space and administrative offices, creating a weighty foundation. In contrast, the dormitory floors above are sheathed in rippling fins of frosted glass, dramatically lit at night, representing the institution's dynamic, forward-looking character. The fins also offer ample privacy and daylight for students while screening dorm rooms from public view. The recessed floor in between contains the student reading room, which stretches across the facade and spills onto a broad balcony.

Inside, playful modern elements speak to the building's youthful population: an abstracted map of the city in laser-cut steel, pops of hot pink and crimson in soft furnishings, and LED accent lighting that sets walls awash in the university's signature purple. The interconnecting stair, featured on the facade, gives life to the building and provides light for two levels below grade, where a 160-seat auditorium and seminar rooms are housed. And to maximize the site's slim footprint, Hickok Cole topped the project off—literally—with sustainable vegetation covering more than 75 percent of the building's roof, helping it achieve LEED Gold certification.

Clockwise from right:
In the reading room, a powdercoated perforated-metal ceiling treatment mimics the zigzag of the exterior fins; the architects achieved this column-free volume by supporting the residence levels above via a superbeam from the roof. The corner staircase, connecting lower-level educational facilities with upper administrative floors, is edged in LED strip lighting. In the four-person dorm suites, kitchen cabinetry is sleek plastic laminate. The lobby's map mural, made of laser-cut steel, was treated to a high-gloss powdercoating.

PROJECT TEAM YOLANDA COLE, LAURENCE CAUDLE, SEAN WAYNE, KERRON MILLER, JEFFREY A. LOCKWOOD, RHEA VAFLOR, TODD D. MARTIN, ROSA ZLOTKOVSKY, CAMEO ROEHRICH, NATALIE HNATIW, SARAH BARR
MEP ENGINEER GIRARD ENGINEERING
STRUCTURAL ENGINEER FERNANDEZ AND ASSOCIATES
CIVIL ENGINEER AMT ENGINEERING
LANDSCAPE DESIGN PARKER RODRIGUEZ
LIGHTING CONSULTANT GEORGE SEXTON ASSOCIATES
AUDIOVISUAL CONSULTANT MILLER BEAM & PAGANELLI
PHOTOGRAPHY ADRIAN WILSON, ANICE HOACHLANDER (4)

www.hickokcole.com

78,800 sf
12 floors
LEED Gold certified

1 MEETING ROOM

2 STAIRCASE

3 WORKSTATIONS

4 OFFICES

5 CORRIDOR

6 READING ROOM

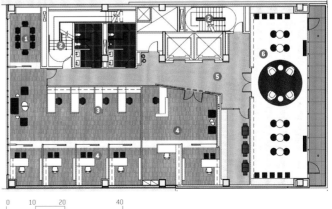

0   10   20   40

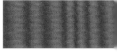

Wid Chapman Architects

EDUCATIONAL HOUSING SERVICES NEW YORKER HOTEL STUDENT RESIDENCE, NEW YORK

Clockwise from right:
A breakout lounge positioned between existing columns clad in reclaimed timber is further delineated with a drywall ceiling soffit and color-blocked nylon carpet. Durable finishes, fixtures, and furnishings—these powdercoated-steel stools among the latter—animate the kitchen. Custom decals that embellish the glass separating two living rooms mimic the motifs painted on the columns behind. Budget-friendly MDF gets a high-color makeover in a custom bookcase. Chapman's custom wall covering in the elevator lobby.

Principal Wid Chapman created a building within a building in his transformation of the 15th floor of a 1930s hotel into a mini metropolis of student housing. The design team needed to provide individual and group study spaces, recreation zones, and cooking and dining areas—all with a youthful spin. Strong colors, graphic elements, and a dose of retro flair give the off-campus residence a playful sensibility. The team clad existing columns in reclaimed wood that a local artist hand-painted with geometric patterns. Similar shapes and colors crop up in the elevator bank's eco-friendly PVC-free wall coverings, custom designed by Chapman.

In the common room, structural columns blocked sight lines, creating unwieldy spaces. Chapman managed to convert them into assets, however—here, by tucking a television nook in sky-blue and citrus-yellow color blocking within a configuration of columns. The latter hue reappears alongside gray in the adjacent library, in a zany skewed-angle bookshelf as mod as the chairs beside it.

For high-traffic areas, durability was a major concern, addressed in part by kitchen cabinets made with an aluminum-composite paneling typically used on exteriors. Because millennials require the latest technology, iPad stations abound; Chapman also installed Apple's wireless AirPlay so students can stream music straight from their cell phones—whatever, whenever, and wherever they like.

PROJECT TEAM WID CHAPMAN, JEFFREY LUONG, AARON LEE, CARMEN SANTAELLA
GENERAL CONTRACTOR SIDWELL CONSTRUCTION
MILLWORK NYC BUILDERS
MEP ENGINEER M. CHETRIT CONSULTING ENGINEERS
LIGHTING CONSULTANT DESIGN ONE LIGHTING
PHOTOGRAPHY PAUL JOHNSON

www.widchapman.com

24,000 sf

A&E Architects and Staat Creative Agency

STUDENT HOTEL AMSTERDAM, NETHERLANDS

Dreary dorm rooms are *so* over. That is, if you're studying at the University of Amsterdam or the nearby Gerrit Rietveld Academy. Thanks to the combined efforts of four firms, a onetime office complex on the outskirts of town got a crash course on contemporary design—and was transformed into vibrant student housing. This outpost of the hospitality brand Student Hotel Group features 700 furnished bedrooms with en suite bathrooms and shared kitchens, plus access to a restaurant, study hall, and social areas. Most are in a pair of 1968 concrete office blocks converted by A&E Architects. "From the outside, you think they're gray and not very interesting," says senior architect Arend Rutgers. "But it's amazing how much intimacy you can create in this kind of setting." The firm also added a seven-story building in more traditionally Dutch red brick.

Interiors by Staat Creative Agency read more boutique hotel than dormitory. There's even a reception station, in the brand's signature collegiate yellow. The mood turns rustic in the Kitchen, a restaurant that also offers meal plans. Koelhuis Frigo and Jelle Maijer/Environments built the picnic-style tables and benches from scrap wood and added vintage-inspired hanging plants. After breakfast, students can bolt to class on borrowed bicycles stored in the basement.

Clockwise from top: A&E Architects converted two 1968 office buildings into dorms. Bold lettering marks the university dormitory complex. Powdercoated steel mesh encircles the reception window. Near cheeky signage, vintage chairs surround study-hall tables lit by industrial-style pendants. ➤

700 bedrooms

PHOTOGRAPHY KASIA GATKOWSKA
www.aearchitects.com
www.staatamsterdam.nl

Clockwise from above: A chair by Michael Sodeau sits in a deluxe bedroom. A half-moon timber patio enlivens the former office block. Seating by the likes of Harry Bertoia and Alfredo Häberli mingles with old-school billiard tables in the game room. The restaurant tables and benches were custom-built from scrap wood. A vintage neon lightning bolt denotes the game room adjoining reception.

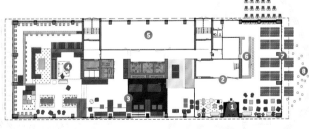

0   20   40   80

1 ENTRY

2 RECEPTION

3 LOBBY

4 LIBRARY

5 FITNESS CENTER

6 BAR

7 RESTAURANT

8 TERRACE

Joel Sanders
Architect

EDUCATION COMMONS, UNIVERSITY OF
PENNSYLVANIA, PHILADELPHIA

College kids have an unshakable, nearly primal desire to sprawl. That was a cornerstone discovery when Joel Sanders undertook rigorous ergonomic research on student study habits. "We found that when they are absorbing information, students do it in a relaxed posture," he explains. "It's not really until they are writing papers that they tend to sit upright." Therefore, he concluded, study halls should offer both options, plus a few in between.

The pet initiative of the university president, the assignment involved converting 7,000 square feet of wasted, empty space—under the bleachers of a venerable redbrick sports stadium—into a wired, flexible study hub. An obvious challenge was the noise generated by the thousands of cheering fans sitting directly overhead during games. In addition, the loftlike volume took an awkward shape, stepping upward as the bleachers did. The ceiling leaked, too, so Sanders lined it with a rain screen painted the same sky blue as the walls. Below, an undulating white canopy evokes clouds while dampening sound.

The space is divided into what Sanders calls "a series of microclimates": the entry, 11 glass-enclosed meeting rooms, and a study hall scattered with armchairs and ottomans. The entry's flooring is the existing concrete slab, polished. Farther in, graphic-patterned carpeting appears—an essential buffer when stretching out is behavior not merely tolerated but encouraged.

Clockwise from left:
The commons is tucked under the bleachers of Franklin Field, the University of Pennsylvania's 1895 stadium. In the study hall, durable nylon carpet pairs with ottomans upholstered in faux suede. The plaster-coated canopy hides mechanical equipment and softens sound from the stadium. ➤

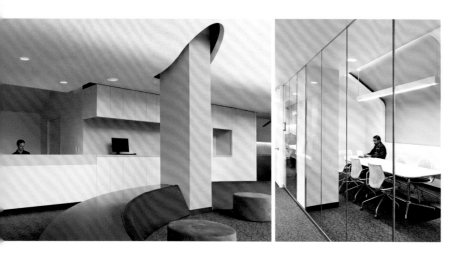

1 ENTRY

2 CONFERENCE ROOM

3 LIBRARIAN'S OFFICE

4 RECEPTION

5 STUDY LOUNGE

6 GROUP STUDY SPACE

0 10 20 40

Clockwise from right: Signage is lacquered wood. One of the 11 glass-enclosed meeting rooms. The study hall is furnished in lounge chairs by Eoos. The volume is 300 feet long, with a width fluctuating between 18 and 28 feet. Yves Béhar designed the task chairs around the Scott Wilson table in this meeting room.

EDUCATION COMMON

7,000 sf

LIGHTING CONSULTANT TILLOTSON DESIGN ASSOCIATES
ACOUSTICAL CONSULTANT METROPOLITAN ACOUSTICS
MEP AHA CONSULTING ENGINEERS
GENERAL CONTRACTOR PAUL RESTALL COMPANY
PHOTOGRAPHY FRANK OUDEMAN/OTTO

www.joelsandersarchitect.com

MHTN
Architects

WILDCAT VILLAGE, WEBER STATE UNIVERSITY
OGDEN, UTAH

Hired to design a trio of student-accommodation buildings for Weber State University, an open-enrollment institution, MHTN questioned whether the firm should conjure a warm, homey feel or a modern, energetic vibe. So the designers hit the books and the streets, teaming with the school's selection committee to review a variety of market trends and to conduct student interviews on the subject. The verdict? Students preferred the latter.

In the buildings—dubbed One, Two, and Three—suites and dormitories incorporating both single- and double-occupancy sleeping quarters are grouped into pods, which are separated by group study areas and common rooms. The result is several neighborhoods at every level, each featuring a designated color that stacks vertically through the building.

Throughout, MHTN achieved a balance between social and solo space. All floors have their own "living room" dedicated to a specific activity—from TV watching and foosball to simulated golf—inspiring students to move between levels, meet peers, and forge new connections. Furniture and finishes are durable and eco-conscious: Steelcase seating, Designtex and Maharam textiles, low-VOC paint and adhesives, and Mohawk carpet tile with high recycled content. All were specified in a vibrant palette of turquoise, amethyst, peach, and yellow, guaranteed to invigorate even the most couch-prone undergrads.

Clockwise from left: A kitchenette fosters gatherings. The mezzanine lounge above the main dining room in Building Two doubles as extra dining space during busy periods. Dining and social space is placed at the hub of resident circulation. The study lounge in Building Two is available to residents of all three Wildcat Village buildings. The school color, purple, forms a primary accent. The social lounge on the top level of Building Three features circular ceiling soffits that echo café tables below; hues were chosen to complement both the signature color and the exterior materials on campus—from golden-buff brick to silvery composite-metal panels.

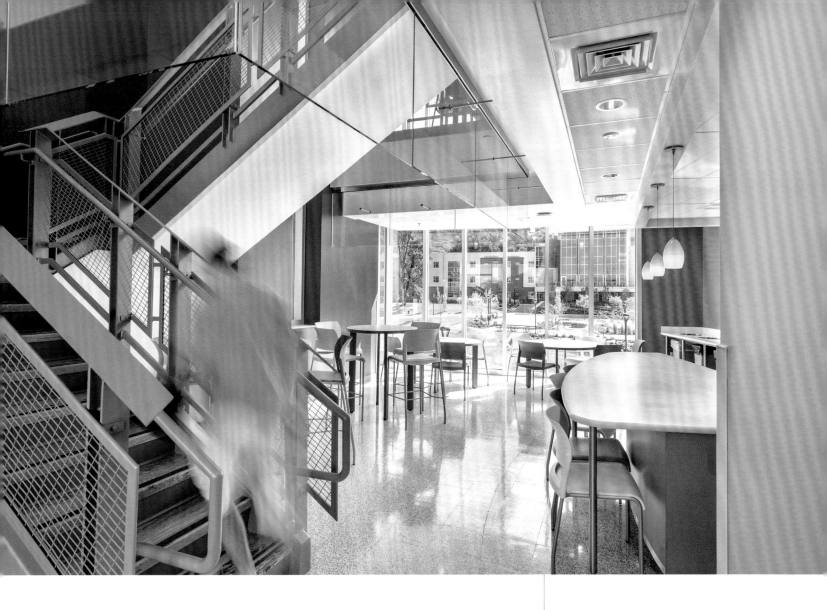

172,000 sf
LEED Silver certified

PROJECT TEAM MICK GAVIGLIO, JOSHUA VEL,
BOBBY STEVENS, DALE THOMAS, MATTHEW
CLINGER, RANDY KNIGHT
GENERAL CONTRACTOR OKLAND CONSTRUCTION
STRUCTURAL ENGINEER ARW ENGINEERS
MECHANICAL COLVIN ENGINEERING & ASSOCIATES
ELECTRICAL ENGINEER ECE
CIVIL ENGINEER GREAT BASIN ENGINEERING
PHOTOGRAPHY TREVOR MUHLER

www.mhtn.com

Robert A.M. Stern Architects

WASSERSTEIN HALL, CASPERSEN STUDENT CENTER AND CLINICAL WING, HARVARD LAW SCHOOL, CAMBRIDGE, MASSACHUSETTS

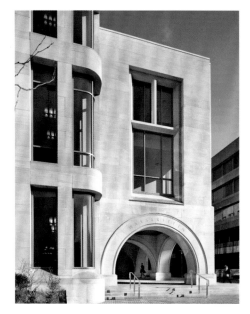

Clockwise from above: Variegated limestone facades with recessed windows and arched entrance porches take cues from the many strands of the law school's architectural legacy. High-performance glazing with an insulating argon-gas layer minimizes heat loss and gain in spaces like the lounge. English oak paneling, Kirkstone slate floors, and door surrounds in Ataija Creme limestone lend warmth to the light-filled gallery. ➤

When the Robert A.M. Stern Architects team arrived to assess the northwest corner of the Harvard Law School campus, they knew they were in for a challenge. Student organizations were scattered thoughout various buildings. Communal space was scarce. The school lacked a true "front door" and central outdoor area all its own. Lastly, though each structure was interesting, the diverse buildings didn't project a coherent identity. The brief was to merge these disparate elements into one gateway building. To be included were classrooms, law clinics, lounges, and a pub, linked via welcoming circulation studded with informal gathering spaces.

The firm's solution was a C-shape building with three wings embracing a rooftop courtyard, which conceals a ground-level loading dock. Synthesizing the campus's varied architectural styles required careful editing and sly invention. The stately five-level limestone edifice—its interiors finished in a palette of stained white oak, polished marble, and oil-rubbed bronze—now bustles with students 24/7. Reading nooks are particularly popular. "One student told me that studying by the fireplace is 'like a storybook come to life,'" says the HLS dean Martha Minow. "My sense is that the project has far exceeded anyone's dreams," adds former dean—and now Supreme Court Justice—Elena Kagan. High praise indeed.

266,000 sf
$167 million construction cost
LEED Gold certified

1 CLASSROOMS

2 BOOKSTORE

3 SERVICE

4 DINING AREA

5 LOUNGE AREA

PROJECT TEAM ROBERT A.M. STERN, GRAHAM S. WYATT, KEVIN SMITH, MELISSA DELVECCHIO, KURT GLAUBER, BRIAN TAYLOR, CHRISTOPHER LASALA, SOPHIA CHA, KIM YAP, DON JOHNSON, DENNIS GEORGE, LORENZO GALATI, OLIVER PELLE, KAVERI SINGH, SUE JIN SUNG, GEORGE DE BRIGARD, TED BRADY, WILLIAM PEREZ, JENNIFER LEE, WILLIAM HOLLOWAY, GRACE CHANG, VICTOR MARCELINO
PHOTOGRAPHY PETER AARON/OTTO

www.ramsa.com

0   20   40   80

Clockwise from right:
The Massachusetts Avenue facade. The cadmium red ceiling and walls in the billiard room make for all-encompassing coziness. Cove lighting, table lamps, and contemporary chandeliers provide multiple sources of illumination in the lounge. Limestone fireplaces are a modern take on a Harvard tradition. Classrooms vary in configuration, from this 90-person tiered style to "cluster classrooms" with breakout zones. A sunny study nook.

Clockwise from right: Bright, saturated paint colors accentuate the building's massive structural columns. The feature wall backdropping the lobby escalator is bedecked with phrases expressing the university's core values. The steel-and-concrete main staircase. The third-floor library, housed in a bridge linking two wings of the building, features café-style seating along with study desks.

The Colorado-based university approached Carrier Johnson with an unusual proposition: convert a city-center shopping mall into classroom facilities. How to make an assemblage of retail stores feel like a college campus? By embracing, rather than effacing, the existing architecture, the design team decided. The building offered—among other great features—abundant industrial details like hefty steel beams, exposed rivets, and full-height windows with custom mullions.

The biggest challenge was preserving the soaring fenestration while addressing HVAC and acoustical concerns. "We wanted to celebrate the height at the window line without having to heat or cool 30-foot volumes," notes principal Danette Ferretti. The solution was to drop the ceiling to 9 feet throughout most of the interior and lift it at the perimeter glazing, where it rises to as much as 21 feet. Enfilades of Louis Poulsen pendants set off the staggered levels, while structural elements left exposed near the windows reflect the building's character. Other interventions, such as a steel-and-concrete staircase, exude similar raw strength.

More rustic highlights include the 42-foot elevator tower, now a dazzling art pillar clad in timber slats and glass panels, and accent walls treated to rust, umber, and citrine tones—evoking the nearby Rockies at sunset.

PROJECT TEAM ERNESTO SANTOS, DANETTE FERRETTI
ASSOCIATE ARCHITECT HEERY INTERNATIONAL
MEP ENGINEER MDP ENGINEERING
STRUCTURAL ENGINEER JIRSA HEDRICK & ASSOCIATES
ACOUSTICAL ENGINEER GEILER & ASSOCIATES
GENERAL CONTRACTOR BOOTS CONSTRUCTION COMPANY
OWNER REPRESENTATIVE BRIDGEPOINT EDUCATION
OWNER PROJECT MANAGER CORPORATE REALTY GROUP
PHOTOGRAPHY COLORADO VISIONS
www.carrierjohnson.com

Carrier Johnson + Culture

UNIVERSITY OF THE ROCKIES, DENVER

EDUCATION CAN IMPROVE LIVES

CELLENCE

"I feel that my education has helped me to serve the marginalized at a level that I never thought possible."
-Debra Stewart, Doctor of Psychology, Educational Leadership and Health and Wellness Psychology Specializations

DEGREE OF SERVICE

ERIENCE LIKE NO OTHER

cultivating tomorrow's thought leaders.

LIZED EDUCATION CAN IMPROVE LIVES.

DYNAMIC

SPECIALIZED EDUCATION CAN IMPROVE LIVES.

LEARNING

52,200 sf

MHTN Architects

**SPENCER FOX ECCLES BUSINESS BUILDING
UNIVERSITY OF UTAH, SALT LAKE CITY**

From top: Mezzanine seating overlooks the double-height fifth-floor café and dining area with adjacent outdoor patio. In the main lobby, an LED-panel art installation shaped like the Great Salt Lake tracks the stock market in real time. ➤

Tasked with translating—and differentiating—the contributions of three major donors within a single structure, MHTN hit on a canny solution: a trio of interconnected pavilions. Each has its own presence, but all are unified by a shimmering aluminum-sheathed box that seems to hover over the supporting brick buildings. The first pavilion, housing mainly classrooms, is defined by a custom bamboo wall nicknamed the Canyon, after the state's distinctive steep slot ravines. The vast honey-color paneled wall, tipped at a slight angle, runs both vertically—from the basement to the eighth level—and horizontally, the length of the building. For every lecture room extending off this spine, there are two smaller, facing rooms—a simple but handy configuration producing abundant flexible meeting space close to classes.

The dramatic landscape of southern Utah provided imaginative fodder for the contemporary design. Throughout, bridges, balconies, and mezzanine levels allude to canyon nooks and crannies. Glass railings bordering the mezzanines dispense with visual barriers, and full-height windows capitalize on views of the Wasatch Mountains and Salt Lake Valley. Now the business school's physical space meshes with its progressive program—all the better to inspire the decision makers of tomorrow.

Clockwise from right: *The nine-story building incorporates three pavilions. Composed of custom glass fiber–reinforced gypsum, the auditorium ceiling is grooved to deflect sound from the front of the space to the back. Bamboo slats of varying sizes produce a striking striated effect on a feature wall running the length of the building interior. Saturated colors borrow from the state's signature rock formations. An amphitheater-style lecture hall with sustainable-wood ceiling offers a view of city lights.*

0 20 40   80

1 LECTURE HALL
2 TRADING FLOOR
3 STUDENT SERVICES
4 AUDITORIUM

188,600 sf
$72 million construction cost
$4 million furnishings cost
LEED Silver certified

PROJECT TEAM PEGGY McDONOUGH, BOBBY STEVENS, BRENT AGNEW, MICK GAVIGLIO, ANGELICA PAVONI,
JEFF JUIP, RUI BENTO DE MORAIS, MATTHEW CLINGER, DON WILLIAMS, CHRISTIANE PHILLIPS
PHOTOGRAPHY TREVOR MUHLER

www.mhtn.com

science and technology

State-of-the-art research is best conducted in a state-of-the-art facility, but the demands of scientific inquiry often lead to a prioritization of function over form.

Here, though, performance and aesthetics have equal billing. Whether a STEM high school or a mobile research station on an Antarctic ice shelf, these structures celebrate the engineering and inventiveness that went into their conception—and that the spaces were designed to nurture. Most incorporate advanced sustainability practices, and all engender a sense of community and invite cross-disciplinary dialogue. Hence the recurrence of gathering spaces, touchstones in the natural world, and high-tech media walls used to promote and announce the activities within. *Research put into practice.*

Hugh Broughton Architects and AECOM

HALLEY VI RESEARCH STATION, ANTARCTICA

Clockwise from above: *Hugh Broughton Architects, collaborating with AECOM engineers, won the design competition for the British Antarctic Survey's Halley VI mobile research station on the Brunt Ice Shelf. Pierre Paulin lounge chairs accent the living area. A cherry-veneer staircase links the two levels in the main module. Bedrooms feature Michele De Lucchi task lamps on built-in maple-veneer desktops. The modules' hydraulic legs extend to lift the units above the rising snow.* ➤

Location, location, location. How about atop floating ice—comfortably thick, of course—only 900 miles from the South Pole? That's what the Halley VI research station, an eight-year joint project between Hugh Broughton Architects and AECOM engineers, does. It's composed of seven 1,600-square-foot modules housing laboratories and bedrooms, plus a 5,100-square-foot main module dedicated to community living. The modules are arranged desert-caravan style, each encased in an 8-inch-thick composite "skin" so tightly insulated that heat thrown off by the electric generators is enough to warm the entire station. Halley VI also boasts previously unheard-of Antarctic amenities: generous dimensions intended to combat claustrophobia, a soaring recreation area,

expanses of high-performance glazing for unrivaled views of the aurora australis, a palette of calming or invigorating hues customized by a color consultant who's also a practicing psychologist, and "alarm clocks" that employ simulated daylight to gently wake you—and adjust your blood-cell balance during the three winter months of total darkness. Previous research stations were "seen as ultimately pragmatic," Broughton says. "Our starting point was to create spaces of joy."

Halley VI is also mobile. Because the ice shelf moves toward the sea at a rate of 1,300 feet a year, the station rests on legs equipped with skis that make it towable. The legs are hydraulic, capable of extending to keep their independent yet connected modules above the snow line.

16,300 sf
$40 million project cost
8 years to complete

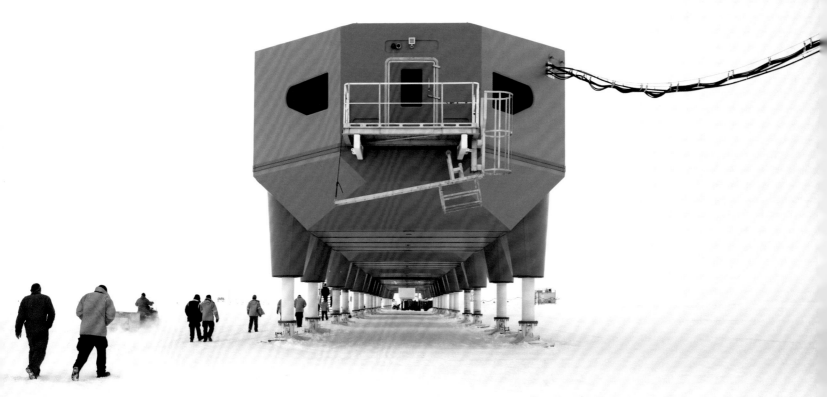

"In Antarctica, 'life-critical' is a condition that enters every design decision you make" —HUGH BROUGHTON

The air temperature around Halley VI can fall to minus 69 degrees Fahrenheit. The perpendicular orientation of the modules to the prevailing wind—which blows up to 100 miles an hour—reduces snow buildup underneath. ➤

Clockwise from left:
Interior colors were
chosen to invigorate
or calm. Daylight,
when available,
enters the recreation
area through
high-performance
glass and aerogel
insulation panels.
The Lebanese cedar
veneer behind the
spiral staircase
introduces a
reassuring scent
otherwise absent
from the environment.
Air-traffic control
shares a module with
other operations. In
the cafeteria, David
Rowland chairs flank
tables topped in
plastic laminate. The
steel skis attached to
the module legs allow
the station to
move like a train.

HUGH BROUGHTON ARCHITECTS PROJECT TEAM HUGH BROUGHTON,
SARAH BESLEY, PHILIP WELLS, LUCA RENDINA, GRENVILLE HERRALD,
MAX MARTIN, ADAM KNIGHT
STRUCTURAL ENGINEERS AECOM
COLOR CONSULTANT COLOUR AFFECTS
CLADDING CONSULTANT BILLINGS DESIGN ASSOCIATES
WOODWORK JOYCE & REDDINGTON
STAIR CONTRACTOR LEWES DESIGN CONTRACTS
GENERAL CONTRACTOR GALLIFORD TRY
PHOTOGRAPHY JAMES MORRIS

www.hbarchitects.co.uk
www.aecom.com

1 LOUNGE

2 DOUBLE-HEIGHT SPACE

3 GYMNASIUM

4 PLANT ROOM

5 STAIRCASE

0   10   20   40

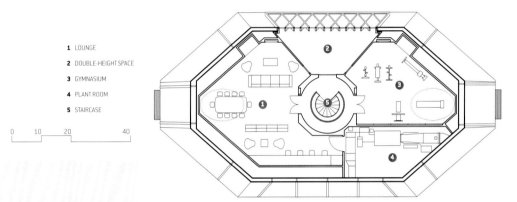

310,000 sf
$112 million project cost
80 research labs
LEED NC Gold registered
49% locally sourced materials
47% energy cost reduction

B+H Architects

ED LUMLEY CENTRE FOR ENGINEERING INNOVATION
UNIVERSITY OF WINDSOR, ONTARIO

For this ground-up state-of-the-art research hub, B+H Architects envisioned a beautifully restrained yet hardworking building that celebrates its inner workings at every turn. Unifying the interior is a palette of high-performance glass, honey-toned laser-milled Douglas fir panels, and Glulam beams and columns—the latter left gloriously exposed. Typically concealed elements, from electrical conduits to water pipes, are likewise on full view. So, too, are the hollow concrete-slab floors and walls, which store thermal energy generated by the sun, the building equipment, and the occupants. The structure itself even serves as a teaching tool: High-tech gadgets, such as sensors that monitor heat lost through the roof, provide live data on the center's operation.

At the heart of the building is an airy atrium that functions as a crossroads between departments. It's spanned by four bridges furnished with informal seating; each skywalk demonstrates a unique engineering principle and construction technique. Forming a vivid backdrop to public areas is a 36-foot-high green wall. More than 1,500 plants—representing 14 varieties—make up the vertical garden, their leaves arranged in wide diagonals of purple and green. Not just a showpiece, the garden offers serious health benefits: Integrated with the ventilation system, the plants "scrub" 10,000 cubic feet of air per minute, absorbing carbon dioxide and VOCs. For a heartier dose of fresh air, students can head to the landscaped rooftop terrace and do homework alfresco.

Clockwise from top: Anchoring the three-level skylit atrium is a biofilter wall composed of an array of specially selected plants. High-performance glazing on the north facade. Laser-milled Douglas fir brings warmth to a lecture theater.

PROJECT TEAM DOUGLAS BIRKENSHAW, KEVIN STELZER, ALAN FRASER, LUCA VISENTIN, GUY PAINCHAUD

STRUCTURAL CONSULTANTS HALSALL ASSOCIATES, ALEO ASSOCIATES

SUSTAINABLE DESIGN CONSULTANT HALSALL ASSOCIATES

MECHANICAL CONSULTANTS SMITH AND ANDERSEN, COLLINS-FERRERA ENGINEERING

ELECTRICAL CONSULTANTS CROSSEY ENGINEERING, SMYLIE & CROW ASSOCIATES

COST CONSULTANT TTCM2R

LANDSCAPE ARCHITECT QUINN DESIGN ASSOCIATES

CONTRACTOR PCR CONTRACTORS

PHOTOGRAPHY TONI HAFKENSCHEID (1, 2, 4–7), DAN REAUME (3)

www.bharchitects.com

1 LEARNING SPACE

2 CAFÉ AND STUDENT SPACES

3 ATRIUM

4 AERODYNAMIC TESTING

5 STRUCTURAL ANALYSIS LAB

6 INDUSTRIAL COURTYARD

7 LABORATORIES

0   20   40   80

Clockwise from top left: Structural elements—such as the ceiling beams in a lecture hall—remain exposed. The hollow concrete slabs forming the interior structure absorb and retain heat effectively. The exterior precast concrete cladding is tinted and textured to add warmth to the facade. In the atrium, bridges furnished with casual pieces abet departmental cross-pollination.

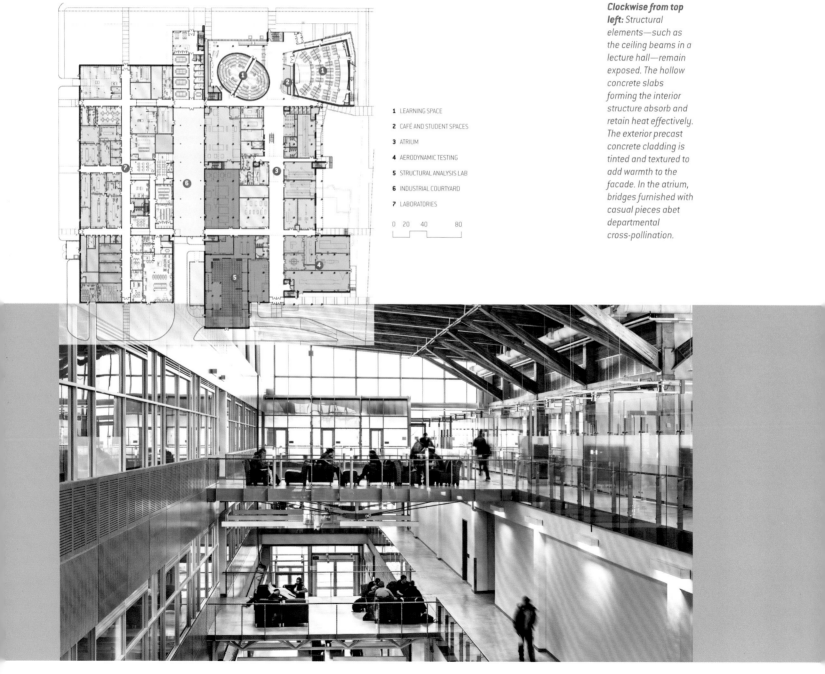

Cuningham Group Architecture

INSTITUTE OF SCIENCE AND TECHNOLOGY
AURORA, COLORADO

Cherry Creek School District 5 aimed for the stars when embarking on its mission to create a university-caliber science, technology, engineering, and mathematics facility (STEM, in educational parlance) for local middle- and high school students. With a little help from Cuningham Group Architecture, the client achieved just that. The district even gained a laboratory sophisticated enough for real-world scientific research and secured a research grant from NASA to study components for space travel.

Mirroring the facility's sky-high ambitions, the design team embedded STEM motifs throughout the interior: An LED installation depicts a star map, a sculptural column takes the shape of a double helix, fenestration patterns derive from the Fibonacci series, latitude and longitude coordinates embellish floors, and details on glazing suggest microchips.

The masterstroke, though, is that the building itself functions as a teaching tool. Note the light-collecting rooftop heliostat, with a platform for conducting experiments, and the "energy dashboard" that allows classrooms to chart consumption—and compete for most efficient. The integration of learning opportunities has been so seamless, it's not unusual to encounter students measuring or recording building features for an assignment.

Surely students are learning just as much about the principles of good design as they are about science.

Clockwise from top left: A rooftop Sundolier light-collecting device coaxes sunshine down a pipe and into the central stairway. Cast into the epoxy terrazzo floors are 2-inch-wide brushed-stainless-steel bars that represent latitude and longitude. Hallways are lined with murals of renowned scientists, mathematicians, and technologists. Situated between the existing Prairie Middle School and Overland High School buildings, the structure services students from both schools. An overhead LED star map illuminates the lobby. Pristine true-white paint on walls and ceiling helps optimize daylight.

PROJECT TEAM PAUL HUTTON, TODD VANDENBURG, HEATHER BOCK, MARK CORMIER, JEANETTE M. TORRENTS, DOUGLAS DUNKIN, MARK WEST, GARY SCHAFFER, SCOTT MILLER, NANCY WHITE, DENNIS DISNEY, JAMES HOPPER
PHOTOGRAPHY FRANK OOMS

www.cuningham.com

58,000 sf
$13.8 million project cost

Belzberg Architects

McKINNON CENTER FOR GLOBAL AFFAIRS
OCCIDENTAL COLLEGE, LOS ANGELES

After winning a strictly idea-based competition for the redo of century-old Johnson Hall, Hagy Belzberg stripped the building back to the studs and conceived it as a space that "instead of just housing technology *is* technology," in his words. The nexus of the entire project is the large-scale media wall in the lobby, a gently folded plane in slumped glass sandwiching a layer of vinyl printed in one of two graphic patterns. The wall has dual kinetic aspects. The first incorporates 10 monitors that showcase student- and faculty-generated content created with a proprietary app called Global Crossroads, which highlights the depth and dimension of work being explored on campus and around the globe. The second involves computer-controlled LEDs whose colors oscillate in response to the dynamic content being shown across the displays. Blues, purples, or oranges sweeping across the wall announce that someone is mounting a presentation. "As the tones move, they create a moment," the architect says. "It's like the curtain going up on an old-time movie."

However, when it came to the auditorium (originally a chapel), Belzberg traded his technology hat for a preservation one. During demolition, he discovered the ceiling beams had been painted with a floral motif and sealed over long ago, so he painstakingly restored them. History, after all, is integral to a well-rounded education.

From opposite:
Kane Design Studio's modular lounge seating fills the lobby at the McKinnon Center for Global Affairs. An interactive media wall is the dominant feature of the lobby. ➤

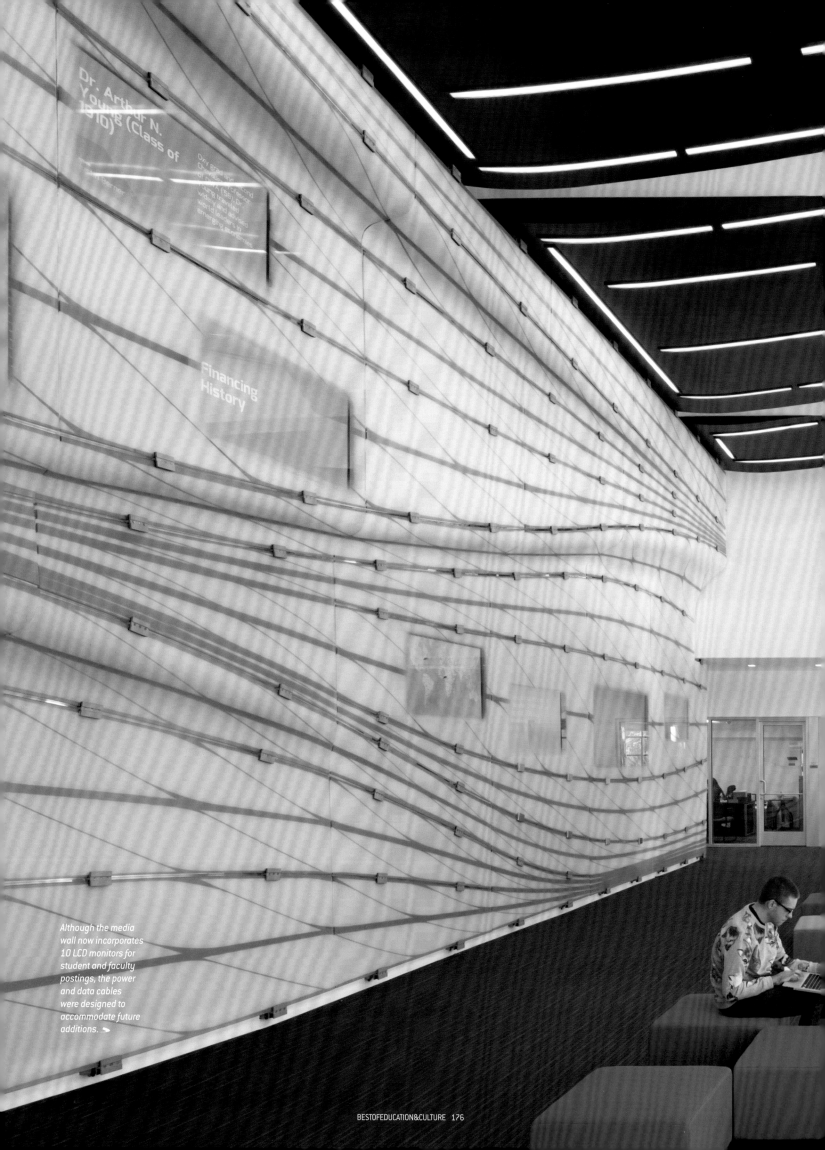

Dr. Arthur N.
Young (Class of
1910)

Financing
History

Although the media wall now incorporates 10 LCD monitors for student and faculty postings, the power and data cables were designed to accommodate future additions.

"We conceived a building that instead of just housing technology *is* technology" —HAGY BELZBERG

PROJECT TEAM HAGY BELZBERG, FAIA, DANIEL RENTSCH, SUSAN NWANKPA, CHRIS SANFORD, CORY TAYLOR, CHRIS ARNTZEN, DAVID CHEUNG, ASHLEY COON

INTERACTIVE DESIGN AND DEVELOPMENT SECOND STORY, PART OF SAPIENTNITRO

STRUCTURAL AND GLAZING THORTON TOMASETTI

ACOUSTICAL NEWSON/BROWN

CLIENT PROJECT MANAGERS DAVID SCHWANKE, PATRIC SCHWANKE

MECHANICAL ENGINEER CALIFORNIA ENGINEERING DESIGN GROUP

ELECTRICAL ENGINEER KOCHER SCHIRRA GOHRIZA

HISTORICAL CONSULTANT DAVID KAPLAN

LIGHTING DESIGN HLB LIGHTING, TEAL BROGDEN

GENERAL CONTRACTOR W.E. O'NEIL

OCCIDENTAL COLLEGE JONATHAN VEITCH, DANIEL CHAMBERLAIN, SHERRY SIMPSON DEAN, CHRIS GILMAN, AMOS HIMMELSTEIN, SANJEEV KHAGRAM, MARSHA SCHNIRRING, BRETT SCHRAEDER, JAMES UHRICH

PHOTOGRAPHY IWAN BAAN (1–5), BENNY CHAN/FOTOWORKS (6–8)

www.belzbergarchitects.com

1 OFFICES

2 MEDIA WALL AND LOBBY

3 INNOVATION LAB

4 CLASSROOM

0 10 20 40

40,000 sf

Clockwise from right:
A steel frame supports
the media wall's
25-by-55-foot
expanse. Recycled
polyester wraps
acoustical panels in
the auditorium.
Writable glass lines a
corridor. Gutting
all four levels, totaling
40,000 square feet,
let Belzberg make a
big statement with
an atrium lobby.
During the auditorium
demolition, the
architect discovered
Myron Hubbard Hunt's
original painted
beams and trio of
windows, all long
concealed.

70,000 sf

BIG | Bjarke Ingels Group

PHOENIX OBSERVATION TOWER, ARIZONA

X marks the spot. Or in this case, Danish architect-superstar Bjarke Ingels's pin-like tower concept marks Phoenix, to be precise. To put the Southwestern city on the world map, Ingels dreamed up a spherical tourist attraction for developer client Novawest that combines a vertiginous observation deck and exhibition space with restaurants and retail destinations.

Sluicing through the spine of the 430-foot reinforced-concrete tower, a trio of glass elevators whisk visitors to the zenith: the observation deck. From here they can wend their way down the spiraling deck's gentle grade, taking in 360-degree views of the desert sky and downtown cityscape. Alternating between open-air and enclosed, the corkscrew promenade varies in width, expanding midway to more generous proportions.

Whether you see an ode to Saturn, a lollipop, a honey dipper, a Neolithic symbol, or a nod to the Guggenheim Museum's famed helical walkway, one thing's certain— if built, the tower will transform the local skyline forever... icon status guaranteed.

Clockwise from above: BIG's design riffs on the Guggenheim's spiral walkway. If built, the tower will be Phoenix's second tallest. Three elevators will carry visitors up the reinforced-concrete core. The spiral promenade provides wraparound views of the desert. Seating and exhibitions dot the observation deck.

PROJECT TEAM BJARKE INGELS, THOMAS CHRISTOFFERSEN, IANNIS KANDYLIARIS, THOMAS FAGAN, AARON HALES, OLA HARIRI, DENNIS HARVEY, BEAT SCHENK
STRUCTURAL CONSULTANT MKA
LOCAL ARCHITECT GENSLER
SUSTAINABILITY CONSULTANT ATELIER10
LANDSCAPE CONSULTANT TENEYCK
DEVELOPER NOVAWEST
www.big.dk

121,000 sf
LEED Gold certified

HDR

**AGRICULTURAL SCIENCES BUILDING
(AGRS) AT UTAH STATE UNIVERSITY,
COLLEGE OF AGRICULTURE AND
APPLIED SCIENCES, LOGAN, UTAH**

Visitors flying into Utah's Logan-Cache Airport glimpse a patchwork of emerald and wheat hues, each square demarcating the farming plots that form the backbone of the regional economy. Visitors to the state university's Agricultural Sciences Building, on the other hand, behold this scene as metaphor: a curtain wall in shades of greenish glass that mimics the rhythm and color palette of the county bird's-eye view as it expresses the essence of the research done within the school walls. Credit the inspired scheme to HDR, which provided both the architecture and the engineering design.

A 265-foot-long office bar and a four-story laboratory block daylit by a vast central atrium make up the new teaching and research facility. The agrarian theme so finely honed on the exterior continues indoors, where wall panels infilled with natural plant materials help identify departments. Limestone floors, fine wood cabinetry, natural fibers, and leather furniture exude a rustic chic more common to high-end hospitality projects. Luxurious? Definitely. And sustainable, too. The final coup: HDR surpassed the client's goal of LEED Silver certification, attaining the much-coveted Gold.

Clockwise from left:
Solar panels above windows both provide shade and produce energy, while operable windows improve air quality and reduce energy consumption. A pale palette helps coax natural light farther into the building.
All interior flooring, coatings, adhesives, and composite wood products contain low amounts of VOCs, contributing to a healthier environment. Glass-enclosed study rooms perch on the second floor, above the four-story skylit atrium.
To make way for the construction of this expanded facility, in which teaching and research would be co-located in one flexible and collaborative environment, Utah State University demolished an outdated existing building.

PROJECT TEAM BRIAN K. NORKUS, BRIAN KOWALCHUK, SHAUN SALAZAR, KIM SHERMAN, MARTIN FARACH, KELLY HARTSHORN,
DAVID DANIELSON, JAMES WERMES, KEVIN KOSOR, DANIEL KILLIAN, DENNIS PATNODE, JOHN VALENCIA
PROGRAMMING CRSA
LANDSCAPE ARCHITECT MGB+A
CIVIL ENGINEER CACHE LANDMARK ENGINEERING
STRUCTURAL ENGINEER DUNN ASSOCIATES
PHOTOGRAPHY PAUL RICHER

www.hdrinc.com

190,000 sf
LEED Gold certified

Francis Cauffman

SAUNDERS RESEARCH BUILDING, CLINICAL AND TRANSLATIONAL SCIENCE INSTITUTE, UNIVERSITY OF ROCHESTER, NEW YORK

The belief that scientists and clinicians working across disciplines can more effectively develop treatments and cures guided this new medical facility's design; in it, researchers and medical staff previously scattered across 11 sites are united under one roof. Design firm Francis Cauffman dubbed the ethos "bench to bedside."

"We wanted the design to promote an exchange of ideas," says principal James Crispino. So to increase chance "bump-ins" and spark collaboration, the firm created a three-story atrium linked by a glass-balustrade stair that promotes interdisciplinary traffic between break rooms, conference rooms, and research labs. The atrium's common areas encourage informal conversations; for work spaces, Francis Cauffman did away with dark, windowless labs, championing instead an open floorplan with generous bays and ceilings. Daylight was key to both reducing energy consumption and providing a healthy environment. Workstations for the 11 research departments line the building perimeter while central offices and meeting rooms are enclosed in glass, rather than drywall, to maximize daylight penetration.

From the outset, the university's goal was to raise the bar in terms of green design—although medical research facilities' 24/7 high energy consumption makes achieving LEED certification a heavy lift. Moreover, being in upstate New York, the building must contend with a temperature gap of almost 100 degrees between the warmest summer day and the coldest winter one. Even so, Francis Cauffman succeeded in creating the very first LEED Gold building on the UR campus.

SAUNDERS RESEARCH BUILDING

Clockwise from right:
Offices are arranged in blocks that run perpendicular to the window walls.
An exterior view.
A three-story central atrium stair links common spaces.
The height and width of fenestration varies, with taller windows on the north elevation to account for lower levels of indirect daylight. ➤

265

Clockwise from top: *The Saunders Research Building shares its new main lobby, finished with acoustical wood panels and a terrazzo floor, with the adjacent School of Nursing—a direct relationship that reinforces the institute's "bench to bedside" mission. Workstations feature Herman Miller furnishings. Café countertops are composed of solid surfacing. The exterior contrasts brick and cast stone with glass curtain-wall elements. Atrium stair treads are sheathed in vinyl. The reception desk is clad in quarter-sliced beech panels that play off the bright back wall.*

MEP ENGINEER BARD, RAO + ATHANAS
STRUCTURAL ENGINEER BERGMANN ASSOCIATES
COST ESTIMATING DAVIS LANGDON
ACOUSTICAL CONSULTANT CERAMI ASSOCIATES
LIGHTING DESIGN GEORGE SEXTON ASSOCIATES
CONSTRUCTION MANAGER LECHASE CONSTRUCTION
PHOTOGRAPHY CHRIS COOPER

www.franciscauffman.com

1 OFFICES
2 BREAK ROOM
3 STAIRCASE
4 CONFERENCE ROOM

0   20   40   80

WHR Architects

UNIVERSITY OF TEXAS HEALTH SCIENCE CENTER (UT HEALTH) SCHOOL OF DENTISTRY AT HOUSTON

In designing a world-class teaching clinic for a longtime client, WHR had a dual mandate: to create a state-of-the-art learning environment and to provide a positive patient experience...with a touch of Southern hospitality. The firm delivered with a scheme at once functional and restful.

Soft-spoken hues instill calm in the reception and clinics; a brighter palette enlivens classrooms and labs. To enhance patient comfort, safety, and satisfaction, the scheme incorporates numerous evidence-based-design best practices, from visual-privacy barriers to beneficial distractions like information monitors above patient chairs.

WHR envisioned a wide variety of teaching environments: tiered fixed-seat classrooms, flexible flat-floor rooms, and advanced simulation labs; one surgical room even features a human-patient simulator. Similarly cutting-edge are study spaces in which standing-height Steelcase Media:scape tables—accompanied by Haworth stools—allow laptop users to share their screen's content with peers working remotely.

The WHR design team wasn't afraid to change direction when inspiration struck. Take the outdoor plaza. What was initially conceived as an angular courtyard reiterating the building's clean-lined geometry developed into a more organic and sustainable design that instead contrasts with the orthogonal architecture. Another inspired move was the repurposing of pink granite cladding from the original UT dental-school building into a conference table and credenza top for the dean's office—a sweet touch, indeed.

Clockwise from right: Globe lanterns suspended from the double-height lobby ceiling provide an ambient glow. Durable, low-emitting finishes promote a healthy environment throughout. Curtain-wall glazing floods the lobby with natural light. The new building, a mid-rise structure of brick and glass, was sited to maximize north-south exposure.

300,000 sf
6 stories

PROJECT TEAM MARY LE JOHNSON, AIA, ASID, LEED AP; JEFF CHITTENDEN, AIA; JOHN SMITH, AIA, LEED AP; CYNTHIA LABELLE, AIA; ROSEANN PISKLAK, RID, IIDA, AAHID, LEED AP; REBECCA WEEMS, IIDA, LEED AP; MIGUEL VILLARREAL
PHOTOGRAPHY GEOFFREY LYON

www.whrarchitects.com

sacred spaces

These houses of worship uplift the spirit and ground the soul. They transcend earthly bounds with awe-inspiring elements—vaulted ceilings, sky-high windows—while telegraphing a humble, communal mien via natural finishes and multifunctional layouts. Whether spare and ethereal or opulent and layered, certain features prevail, such as a heightened sense of materiality and sublime sculpting of illumination. From a New York synagogue with a twinkling dome to an earthquake-proof cardboard cathedral on a South Pacific island, all are utterly transcendent. *The pursuit of the spiritual never looked so divine.*

52,000 sf
5 levels
LEED pending

Clockwise from left:
The glass facade's stone frame conveys the protective covering for the Torah and the tabernacle within. Rustic basalt stone in the lobby recalls the Wailing Wall. Biblical wood species, such as the lobby's lightly stained Cedar of Lebanon, speak to Jewish history. A circular sanctuary allows the Modern Orthodox congregation to pray in the round, reinforcing the sense of unified community; the gently convex ceiling soffit enhances the twinkling of embedded lights.

CetraRuddy

LINCOLN SQUARE SYNAGOGUE, NEW YORK

From its humble beginnings in an Upper West Side apartment in 1964 to a 52,000-square-foot structure in 2013, Lincoln Square Synagogue has traveled a long way—even though the new premises are just a block from the old. "Formalistically, we took our inspiration from the Torah," CetraRuddy associate principal Theresa Genovese says of the building's eastern facade. Five wavelike horizontal ribbons, created with 5,000 square feet of custom glass panels, pay homage to the sacred scroll. Bronze polyester fabric sandwiched between the glass sheets recalls ancient parchment and, together with a frit coating on the interior layer, diffuses light and provides privacy from the bustling streetscape.

Throughout, cultural references abound. Glass enfolds the circular sanctuary, where a convex ceiling of 613 LEDs—one for each religious commandment/mitzvah—approximates a starry desert sky. Basalt stone clads the lobby's floors and walls, the latter detailed with varying panel sizes and reveals that reference the undulations of prayer shawls. Cedar of Lebanon, a wood used in ancient temples, appears in the form of doors, cabinetry, and pews. Additionally, the front canopy, in blackened bronze, is an abstract version of the Hebrew letter *resh*, a symbol for beginning—fitting for an entry. It's architecture as ultimate metaphor, and a successful one at that.

PROJECT TEAM JOHN CETRA, NANCY RUDDY, THERESA GENOVESE, BRANKO POTOCNIK,
JASON BOURGEOIS, JOSEPH LIBRIZZI, SEAN HSU, CHRISTOPHER MUELLER
PHOTOGRAPHY DAVID SUNDBERG/ESTO (1, 3–5, 7, 9–11),
THERESA GENOVESE (2, 6, 8)

www.cetraruddy.com

0   10   20   40

1 MAIN STAIRCASE

2 LOBBY

3 SANCTUARY

4 CORRIDOR

5 OFFICES

6 RESTROOMS

Clockwise from right: Another view of the lobby. A curvilinear central staircase echoes the form of the Torah scroll. Custom carpeting was hand-loomed for the sanctuary. The number of windows in the front doors allude to the 12 original tribes of Israel. The lobby's western-facing window is an abstraction of prayer shawls; energy-efficient glazing reduces heat gain. The glass-encased fabric panels of the facade continue into the main lobby. The staircase connects the ground-floor sanctuary to the upper floor—housing the Beit Midrash (study hall), outdoor terrace, and classroom spaces—and the lower, with its ballroom and kitchens.

HGA

LAKEWOOD CEMETERY GARDEN MAUSOLEUM AND RECEPTION CENTER, MINNEAPOLIS

Modeled on Paris's Cimetière du Père-Lachaise—the final resting place of Oscar Wilde, Marcel Proust, and Jim Morrison—the Lakewood Cemetery opened in Minneapolis in 1871. It went on to attract prominent "residents" of its own, among them Vice President Hubert Humphrey. However, the nondenominational nonprofit eventually found itself with only 25 of the original 250 acres available for development and a mausoleum nearing capacity. That's when the board of trustees set about determining a master plan. HGA was commissioned to build a mausoleum with aboveground space for more than 10,000 remains, as well as a chapel and lounge for post-service receptions, all set on four landscaped acres.

The resulting two-story structure, with its facade of split-faced gray granite, sits amid towering pines and gnarled oaks. Deeply inset windows and doors moderate the entering sunlight while maintaining privacy for guests, who enter through a pair of glass doors with intricately looping bronze grillwork. The materials palette also features mahogany, marble, and onyx in shades of honey yellow, jade green, and coral pink. Light plays against dark, rough against smooth, in a mix offering mourners both dignity and serenity.

1 GARDEN CRYPTS

2 COMMITTAL CHAPEL

3 MECHANICALS

4 GRIEVING ROOM

5 LOWER FOYER

6 CRYPT ROOM

7 COLUMBARIUM ROOM

8 COLUMBARIUM GARDEN

0 20 40   80

Clockwise from top:
Bocci lights and
mahogany paneling
grace the foyer.
The building sits on
four-acre grounds.
Inset chapel windows
overlook a garden
with linear walkway.
A skylight casts a
natural glow on the
green onyx floor.
The charcoal granite
of the exterior
continues inside.

24,500 sf
2014 AIA National Honor Award
2013 IIDA Best of Competition Award
2013 American Society of Landscape
Architects Award of Excellence

PROJECT TEAM JOAN M. SORANNO, JOHN COOK
MAUSOLEUM CONSULTANT CARRIER MAUSOLEUMS CONSTRUCTION
ACOUSTICAL CONSULTANT KVERNSTOEN, RÖNNHOLM & ASSOCIATES
LANDSCAPING CONSULTANT HALVORSON DESIGN PARTNERSHIP
PLASTERWORK ARMOURCOAT
WOODWORK COMMERICAL MILLWORK
METALWORK ELLISON BRONZE, M.G. McGRATH
GLASSWORK ARCHITECTURAL GLASS ART
STONEWORK COLDSPRING, SANTUCCI GROUP
CURTAIN WALL/SKYLIGHT CONTRACTOR EMPIREHOUSE
TILE CONTRACTOR TOM D. LYNCH
GENERAL CONTRACTOR M.A. MORTENSON COMPANY
PHOTOGRAPHY PAUL CROSBY

www.hga.com

Perched atop one of San Francisco's many steep hills, right beside Golden Gate Park, lies a city landmark: St. Ignatius, a double-spired Jesuit church built in 1914. For the past decade, BraytonHughes Design Studios has spearheaded a renovation of the parish, converting poky confessionals into chapels, adding a gallery for exhibitions of interfaith art, and designing custom furnishings. Throughout, the firm labored to tie the structure's architectural past—a mix of Renaissance, Baroque, and Roman elements—with a contemporary expression.

The chapels, each dedicated to a saint, radiate from an ambulatory encircling the cruciform of nave, transept, and chancel. Every saint's life story is embodied in the design, with impeccable attention to detail. Take the LED lights on the ceiling of the chapel of the Lady of Guadalupe, which precisely replicate the constellations seen the night the saint appeared to the peasant Juan Diego. Or the Chapel of St. Ignatius, where a cast-bronze bust is mounted at the namesake's exact height.

A major move was to reconfigure confessionals to suit the ways that today's Catholic Church relates to its followers. A freestanding screen enables parishioners to either sit privately on one side with the priest on the other, in the venerable tradition of anonymity, or—in a modern twist—bypass the screen altogether and seek counsel face-to-face.

Clockwise from opposite: *New elements, such as stained Macore flooring and a Dutch metal finish on the existing ceiling dome, blend seamlessly with the original painted plaster architecture and Ionic columns. Visible beyond the ambulatory are skylit alcove chapels and a gallery space converted from confessionals. In the Chapel of Our Lady of Guadalupe, LED lights re-create constellations. Cast glass tops the altar in St. Joseph's chapel.* ⤷

BraytonHughes Design Studios

ST. IGNATIUS CHURCH, SAN FRANCISCO

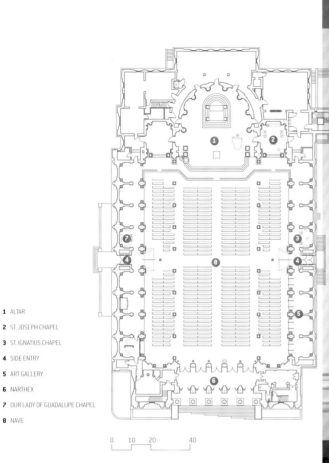

1 ALTAR

2 ST. JOSEPH CHAPEL

3 ST. IGNATIUS CHAPEL

4 SIDE ENTRY

5 ART GALLERY

6 NARTHEX

7 OUR LADY OF GUADALUPE CHAPEL

8 NAVE

0   10   20   40

Clockwise from top:
Leather kneelers and
bench cushions were
custom-designed by
BraytonHughes.
An etched-glass door.
A custom bronze-and-
timber votive stand
in the Chapel of St.
Ignatius. Bronze and
cast glass form a
rose-branch
candelabra in the
Chapel of Our Lady
of Guadalupe.
Computer-aided
sandblasting was
used to engrave an
intricate medallion
on wood in the St.
Ignatius chapel;
above is the ornate
ceiling dome—newly
rendered in a golden
finish—and a
stained-glass panel
that represents the
Holy Spirit descend-
ing toward the
assembly. A new
bronze gate combines
with original marble
flooring and
Corinthian volutes.

3,000 sf

PROJECT TEAM STANFORD HUGHES, JOEL VILLALON, BEATRIZ MARTINEZ WORK,
JACQUELINE LYTLE, KILLIAN O'SULLIVAN, MICHELE KOLBINSKY, VINCENT CHEW
PHOTOGRAPHY JOHN SUTTON

www.bhdstudios.com

Gensler

GENEVIEVE AND WAYNE GRATZ CENTER AT THE FOURTH PRESBYTERIAN CHURCH, CHICAGO

From above:
The cantilevered copper-clad addition houses a 350-person chapel, preschool classrooms, a kitchen and dining facility, lounges and meeting rooms, and a commons. The mazelike limestone floor of the chapel annex—intended for meditation walks—alludes to the neo-Gothic architecture of the main building. ➤

With a congregation fast approaching 6,000, the Fourth Presbyterian Church of Chicago needed more space—the sooner the better. The main challenge was the site's awkward rhombus shape. Gensler's solution: a five-story copper-and-glass addition to one side of the existing 1914 sanctuary and parish house, connected via a double-height commons. To maximize space, the addition's upper stories extend right to the property line, while the footprint contracts at street level to accommodate landscaped lawns and a playground.

The Gratz Center design stays true to the original buildings. Cladding of handcrafted, prepatinated copper panels riff on the copper flashing and downspouts that accent the limestone church. Both materials repeat inside as well, integrating architecture and interiors.

Along the way, the design team—led by principal Lamar Johnson and design director Brian Vitale—unearthed exterior walls covered over in a prior addition. Now decorative limestone detailing hidden for 50-odd years can be viewed through the curtain wall, displayed behind glass like the precious artifact it is. For Vitale, that's what the project is all about. "It is always gratifying," he notes, "to see visitors taking pictures not of our building but of the church through the lens of our building."

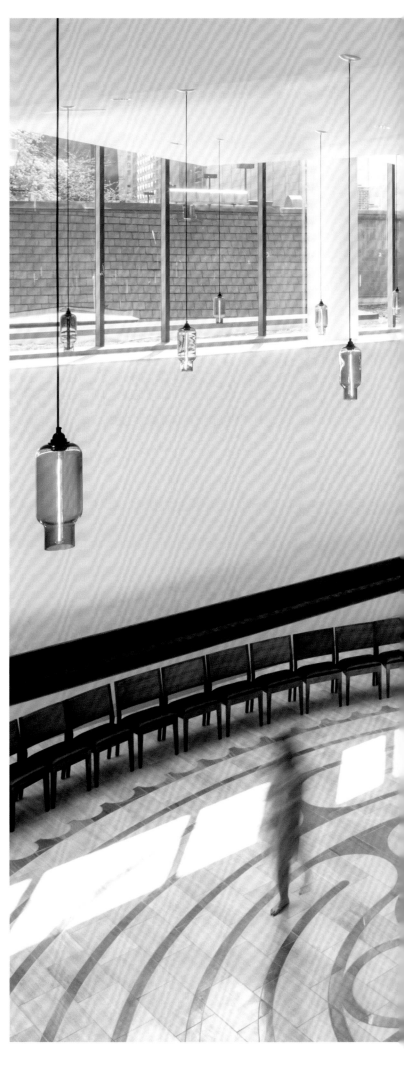

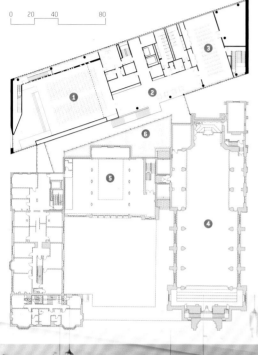

1 CHAPEL

2 LIBRARY

3 MULTI-PURPOSE ROOM

4 SANCTUARY

5 PARISH HOUSE

6 COMMONS

Clockwise from above: The commons joins new and old construction; to the left is the church's original limestone exterior. A custom Lindsey Adelman chandelier hangs in the entry vestibule. The shape and colors of acrylic donor-wall plaques reference the leaded glass windows of an adjacent former chapel, now an events space. In the new chapel, thin apertures distinguish a solid wall in front of the curtain wall; each stripe represents a Christian holy day. Pendants by Jeremy Pyles illuminate the chapel. Cross-bracing in the trefoil-accented Beth Davis Lounge echoes the diagonal lines of the John Hancock Center, seen in the distance.

PROJECT TEAM LAMAR JOHNSON, BRIAN VITALE, TODD HEISER, SCOTT HURST, MARK SPENCER, KARL GUSTAFSON, THOMAS BRAHAM, CARY JOHNSON, STEPHEN KELLOGG
PHOTOGRAPHY RICHARD BARNES
www.gensler.com

79,000 sf
LEED Silver certified

8,300 sf
Pro bono

Shigeru Ban Architects and Warren and Mahoney

PHOTOGRAPHY DAVID HIGGINS
www.shigerubanarchitects.com
www.warrenandmahoney.com

TRANSITIONAL CATHEDRAL CHRISTCHURCH, NEW ZEALAND

When a natural disaster strikes, so does Shigeru Ban, a specialist in emergency architecture. Most recently the *Interior Design* Hall of Famer extended a hand to New Zealand's Christchurch in the wake of the devastating 2011 earthquake that killed 185 people and destroyed over 80 percent of buildings in the city's Central Business District. Among them: the town's 19th-century Gothic-style cathedral, a beloved landmark. In its stead, Ban, working with local architectural firm Warren and Mahoney, proposed an interim replacement made of cardboard, a material suited to quake-prone zones because it flexes under tension.

Forming the walls are eight shipping containers, topped by a steel A-frame covered in 98 polyurethane-coated cardboard tubes, each with a lumber beam inserted for additional strength against high wind loads. Daylight enters the sanctuary via 2-inch gaps between tubes and a triangular window surfaced with colorful film that incorporates imagery from the original cathedral's rose window. Resembling a Maori *marae* in shape, and sheathed with the panels of corrugated polycarbonate common to New Zealand shearing sheds, the structure suits the local vernacular. And this is one house of cards that will not fall. Ironically, the cardboard cathedral is stronger than the stone building it replaced. It's able to withstand 1.2 g's of lateral force—a boon in a city still plagued by daily aftershocks.

Clockwise from opposite: The Transitional Cathedral's congregation worships in custom chairs made of laminated veneer lumber. Polyurethane-coated cardboard tubes reinforced with lumber form the roof. A dramatic exterior view. A detail of the triangular window, whose colorful film references the Holy Trinity.

PROJECT TEAM DANNY CHENG, SIMON KWAN
PHOTOGRAPHY COURTESY OF DANNY CHENG INTERIORS
www.dannycheng.com.hk

2,100 sf

Clockwise from right:
LED and halogen lights delineate the soaring interior, which takes inspiration from the Lamborghini Aventador LP 770. With its sharply peaked roof, the structure bears elements of a traditional chapel. A side view. A reflecting pool encircles the chapel. Danny Cheng conceived the interiors entirely in bridal white, down to the pristine Thassos marble floor.

AUBERGE DISCOVERY BAY HOTEL
WHITE CHAPEL, HONG KONG

White wedding, indeed. The otherworldly serenity of a hotel's nuptial chapel derives from an unlikely source: The layered ceiling recalls the racy lines of a Lamborghini, transposed on a 52-foot-tall A-frame. It surmounts glass walls, offering a spectacular ocean vista, to shelter a space suitable for up to 120 guests, who sit not in standard pews but in rows of fabric-draped chairs. They face a bridal stage with furnishings that are transparent, thereby preserving the view of Hong Kong Disneyland through a wide trapezoidal window.

The seaside site suggested that the chapel be set in a reflecting pool. During daylight hours, the building appears to emerge from the watery depths, while at night the pool becomes a liquid mirror.

Danny Cheng
Interiors and
Simon Kwan
& Associates

JEFF GOLDBERG / ESTO
www.esto.com

TONI HAFKENSCHEID
www.thphotos.com

DAVID HIGGINS
www.davidhiggins.photography

ANICE HOACHLANDER
www.hdphoto.com

PETER AARON / OTTO
www.ottoarchive.com

AKER IMAGING
www.akerimaging.com

TOM ARBAN
www.tomarban.com

LUIS ASÍN
asinluis@yahoo.com

AVOID OBVIOUS
www.avoidobvious.com

IWAN BAAN
www.iwan.com

RICHARD BARNES
www.richardbarnes.net

MARKO BRADICH
www.createrio.com

BENNY CHAN / FOTOWORKS
www.fotoworks.cc

CHUCK CHOI
www.chuckchoi.com

COLORADO VISIONS
www.coloradovisions.com

CHRIS COOPER
www.chriscooperphotographer.com

PAUL CROSBY
www.pcrosby.com

FRANCIS DZIKOWSKI / OTTO
www.ottoarchive.com

KASIA GATKOWSKA
www.kasiagatkowska.com

TIMOTHY HURSLEY
www.timothyhursley.com

PAUL JOHNSON
www.pauljohnsonphotography.com

ERIC LAIGNEL
www.ericlaignel.com

JONATHAN LEIJONHUFVUD
www.jlap.com

DICK LIU
www.trio-photo.com

GEOFFREY LYON
www.glyonphotography.com

BJÖRG MAGNEA
www.bjorgmagnea.com

BYRON MÁRMOL
www.uvuvuv.com

PETER MAUSS / ESTO
www.esto.com

SCOTT McDONALD / HEDRICH BLESSING
www.hedrichblessing.com

DERRYCK MENERE
www.derryckmenere.com

JAMES MORRIS
www.jamesmorris.info

TREVOR MUHLER
www.trevormuhler.com

FRANK OOMS
www.frankooms.com

FRANK OUDEMAN / OTTO
www.ottoarchive.com

RETT PEEK
www.rettpeek.com

CARLOS PÉREZ LÓPEZ
www.chromaticagroup.com

DAN REAUME
www.reaumephoto.com

PAUL RICHER
www.richerimages.com

NIGEL RIGDEN
www.nigrig.com

PAÚL RIVERA / ARCHPHOTO
www.archphoto.com

MIKE SINCLAIR
www.mikesinclair.com

DAVID SUNDBERG / ESTO
www.esto.com

JOHN SUTTON
www.johnsutton.com

MARIANO VADILLO
mariano@a2foto.com

VANNI ARCHIVE
www.vanniarc.com

ADRIAN WILSON
www.interiorphotography.net

photographers
index

EMPOWERING EDUCATION

Discover Juice®, a power delivery system that changes everything.

Empower your facility and learners with the Juice Power System. Juice can power up to eight tables with 16 mobile devices from a single outlet, eliminating the need for an electrician and the clutter of individual power strips. Now furniture and classrooms can be reconfigured in a snap.

Easy, flexible and adaptable

The magnetic connection provides superior safety and quick and easy reconfiguration of furniture and spaces.

Juice offers standard or USB power outlets which can be replaced or reconfigured as your needs change.

The Juice Box has an integrally designed LED light that illuminates to signal that the system is powered and ready to go. Built-in sensors shut down the system when an overload is detected.

Power for devices enables the power to learn. See Juice in action at bretford.com.

CarbonNeutral.com

Technology-enabled furniture for 21st century learning